Marc-Joël Fortelny

Corruption in the Energy Sector

The Dangers of BCEF (Bribery, Crime, Exploitation, Fraud)

Anchor Academic Publishing

Fortelny, Marc-Joël: Corruption in the Energy Sector: The Dangers of BCEF (Bribery, Crime, Exploitation, Fraud). Hamburg, Anchor Academic Publishing 2013

Buch-ISBN: 978-3-95489-192-4
PDF-eBook-ISBN: 978-3-95489-692-9
Druck/Herstellung: Anchor Academic Publishing, Hamburg, 2013

Bibliografische Information der Deutschen Nationalbibliothek:
Die Deutsche Nationalbibliothek verzeichnet diese Publikation in der Deutschen Nationalbibliografie; detaillierte bibliografische Daten sind im Internet über http://dnb.d-nb.de abrufbar.

Bibliographical Information of the German National Library:
The German National Library lists this publication in the German National Bibliography. Detailed bibliographic data can be found at: http://dnb.d-nb.de

Hermannstal 119k, 22119 Hamburg
http://www.diplomica-verlag.de, Hamburg 2013
Printed in Germany

Memorandum

I dedicate this study to all who have helped me along my academic path and to those who will support my future research.
Even though a lot of colleagues got "lost somehow" during my studies, I still want to remember their superficiality as a monument for corrupted behavior in society.

Furthermore, I want to thank my family - who has always encouraged me - and commemorate the departure of my beloved Merlino (*1996-†2013).

In addition, I have to point out Prof. Finsinger, who has rekindled my passion for economics and research, amplified my interest in uncommon topics and shared experience combined with expertise.

Finally, I want to express my gratitude and appreciation to Andrada, my partner in love and in science, who has never forsaken me.

Table of Contents

Table of Figures

Table of Tables

1. Introduction

1.1 Foreword

The energy sector is figuratively seen the motor of not only (real-) economy, technology, machinery, but life itself depending of the definition of standards of society. In such an important field corruption leads to multiple negative results such as a decreased speed in technology research, health issues, decreased life standards, monetary losses, (partially permanent) damages to the environment and also spreads out to other sectors (as higher prices for energy may enforce less competition in various business areas, which is less beneficial from the point of view of total social welfare).
The incentive to use corruption methods is rather high reasoned by (mostly) ineffective counter-measures, powerless regulation agencies, inadequate penalties (or even immunity), a history of "corruption culture" and mostly a disrupted government.

The objective of this research is to depict the energy sector environment regarding the various sources of energy, the correlation of energy mixes, various trends of transition and mainly corruption of these preceding aspects. A view of successful probable and failing counter-measures will also be provided.

The introduction enables a broad outline of deregulation, regulatory agencies and the process of restructuring in aspect to corruption.

A unique part will be the comparison of the general corruption in the public sector of various countries and the perceived corruptive behavior in the energy sector. Considering the setting of the energy sector, namely the attribute of supra-nationality and its cross-linking to the financial sector, the greater cases cannot be limited to countries (or even small time frame).

The definition of corruption will be discussed as well and is absolutely crucial to fully acknowledge results of various methods which cannot always be accredited directly as the main nature of corruption is secrecy.

The probably most interesting part is the collection of extracted key factors where “entry points” of corruption are indicated, analyzed and referenced. A focus on clarification of misinformation is emphasized as well.

> *“Those who corrupt the public mind are just as evil as those who steal from the public purse.”*
>
> - *Adlai Stevenson II, UN Ambassador (1900-1965)*

This study should provide a solid overview of the relation between corruption and the energy sector, numerous cases or certain methods and a few focused and further discussed details.

[1]

[1] http://goo.gl/XAKhQ (last accessed on 24.05.2013)

1.2 Side Remark on Deregulation and Corruption

In the last decades the energy sector has endured vast regulation changes concerning deregulation, liability adaptations and structure – even if most of the parts (inventions like electricity for instance) are, historically seen, quite new like the theory of economic regulation which dates back to the nineteenth century. The main goal of an efficient regulation nowadays is to adapt to the global requirements of a responsive and flexible system.

A regulatory board should not only monitor the regulation methods and their respective usage, but also the environment of the firm, its respective operating sectors, its investments and its long-term strategic planning.

Various examples indicate that deregulation in general may cause different problems, instabilities and even breakdowns. One reason for that is the definition of deregulation, namely, simply put a reduction in monitoring and therefore authority. This results mostly in a tendency to exploit the absence of a certain control level, which enables an entry point for corruption. [2] (Proven by the California case)

> *"California's deregulated power industry, in which producers can sell electricity for whatever the traffic will bear, was supposed to deliver cheaper, cleaner power. But instead the state faces an electricity shortage so severe that the governor has turned off the lights on the official Christmas tree — a shortage that has proved highly profitable to power companies, and raised suspicions of market manipulation. The experience raises questions about deregulation. And more broadly, it is a warning about the dangers of placing blind faith in markets."*
>
> - Paul Krugman (Nobel laureate in economics and Princeton University Professor)

[2] http://business.baylor.edu/Tom_kelly/Californial%20Power.htm (last accessed on 22.02.2013)

Some of these examples and their underlying principles will be analyzed in later chapters. A broad overview of the difficulties that a regulatory institution may encounter should be achieved. The cases of California, Turkey, Ukraine and South America will show that the problems of regulation in fact do not rely upon the simple application of methods and monitoring. The system of an energy market has to be stabilized on all of the different parts of the distribution chain. When the financial market intersects with the energy market the nature of its fluctuations logically produces instabilities such as abundance, which results in profit loss of a firm and shortage which affects the consumer negatively either in a higher price or life standards perceptible, like the oil speculation for instance. There is an academic discordance on this topic.[3]

It has to be mentioned, that energy regardless of its forms should be seen as a "necessity" and not a mere commodity. When compared to a normal product (even if produced by a monopoly) the dependence by society is limited. Therefore the impact of failure is huge and affects in different levels on a global scale the world economy. [4] [5]

1.3 Regulatory Agencies – under constant pressure

The tasks of these institutions are numerous and sophisticated. An absence of influence cannot be guaranteed regardless of the political system, the degree of technological advancement or the level of bureaucracy. The negative side of such an influence is not always "classic" corruption but a circumvention of the regulatory framework. Hence, the regulatory lag must be as little as possible to minimize losses either of the firm or the society. Usually the utility firms are in favor. [6]

---

[3] http://www.risk.net/energy-risk/feature/2232244/academic-battle-rages-over-oil-speculation-high-prices-and-volatility (last accessed on 22.02.2013)

[4] Kilian, Lutz: "The Economic Effects of Energy Price Shocks" University of Michigan (2007), Pg.40

[5] Fortelny, Marc-Joël: "When and how is regulation circumvented in the energy market?", University of Vienna (2013), Pg. 2

[6] http://www.valueline.com/Stocks/Commentary.aspx?id=13098 (last accessed on 22.02.2013)

The main goal of a regulatory agency is to find a regulation that exceeds its costs of appliance by the benefit. Naturally, the costs are two-sided, whereas the direct costs are minuscule and the indirect costs can be extremely high.

The other question is if without regulation the prices would be too high overall and/or the situation would be anti-competitive by meaning of an artificial monopoly, which is rather complicated in a sector of natural monopolies, a strict regulation is necessary in the first place as various scientists favor deregulation.
When an energy sector is privatized, its firms can be bought by private companies usually via a monopoly concession. The decision of which is the most suitable operator is heavily influenced by the rating system (factors are weighted) and the bid sum. [7]

A misdetermination may result in an impossible situation for re-regulation and adaptation to an efficient system. There are various instances of regulatory boards which can be directly linked to a ministry of energy, nature and environment, or rather independent. The controlling areas comprise the direct or indirect setting of the price, the revenues and operating areas of the firm, the investments, quality reassurance and sustainability. The financial market to that extent is far more difficult to control where the major tradeoffs are done by middlemen and not by both ends of the chain.[8]

> *"A McClatchy review of the latest Commitment of Traders report from the Commodity Futures Trading Commission (regulates oil trading) shows that producers and merchants made up just 36 percent of all contracts traded in the week ending Feb. 14 while speculators (who will never take delivery of the oil) made up 64 percent."* [9]

---

[7] can be too high or too low depending on estimations/ expectations that may vary greatly

[8] Fortelny, Marc-Joël: "When and how is regulation circumvented in the energy market?", University of Vienna (2013), Pg. 3-4

[9] http://www.mcclatchydc.com/2012/02/21/139521/once-again-speculators-behind.html (last accessed on 22.02.2013)

1.4 When Structures are reshaped

Without going into too many details, the history of regulation in electricity is relatively brief. In the U.S. the first regulatory agency was already founded in the 1900s and was called Federal Energy Regulatory Commission (FERC) - the definition of an overall energy sector and its regulation followed decades after.

The creation was also based on the necessity of a stable procurement, which was not possible with the occurring franchise system that prevailed the first decades. The FERC´s are different institutions in different states with different rules such as the conduction of transactions regarding electricity and natural gas.
Natural monopolies existed due to the nature of the sector. These resources were considered to be too important to not be regulated. This has changed with the commonly split of the unified monopoly in three subsectors (generation, transmission and distribution) in the 1990´s and tested the strength and authority of the regulation boards.

The European Market has its European Regulators´ Group for Electricity and Gas (ERGEG) and its respective state related regulatory boards like E-Control in Austria and the "Bundesnetzagentur" in Germany. Deregulation or privatization have been controlled by the EU government more or less carefully and as unified as possible – adapted to the market situation and stability.
When compared to the U.S. market privatization it seems private firms have not succeed in having more efficiency and lower prices than state owned utility companies.

> *"By 2000, 24 states and the District of Columbia had passed laws ordering or allowing their monopoly utilities to sell their power plants to other companies or to transfer them to their own unregulated affiliates. But eight years later ten states had repealed or delayed their deregulation laws in response to the California energy crisis of 2000-01 and other problems associated with deregulation."*[10]

---

[10]Slocum, Tyson: "The Failure of Electricity Deregulation: History, Status and Needed Reforms", Public Citizen´s Energy Program (2007), Pg. 6

Average Retail Price of Household Electricity in Rate-Regulated States and Deregulated States Without Rate Caps (cents/kWh)

Residential Customers	2002	2003	2004	2005	2006	2007	Jan-June '08	Average Annual Growth from 2002
38 Rate-Regulated States	7.7	7.9	8.1	8.4	9.1	9.3	9.5	+3.6%
12 Deregulated States Without Rate Caps in 2008	10.3	10.8	11.1	12.1	13.8	14.1	14.2	+5.5%
Difference between rate-regulated and deregulated states	+34%	+37%	+37%	+43%	+52%	+50%	+49%	

Note: The 12 deregulated states are CA, CT, DE, MA, MD, ME, MT, NH, NJ, NY, RI, TX and DC. Deregulated OH and PA are included with regulated states due to existing price caps.

Source: Calculations based on U.S. Energy Information Administration data www.eia.doe.gov/cneaf/electricity/epm/epm sum.html

Table 1: Comparison of the prices between deregulated and rate-regulated states [11]

Privatization has a tendency to be corrupted in the process, especially if the regulatory boards do not have enough political power and independence. Resulting from the calculations of this table, it can be stated that the prices of deregulated states are significantly higher and thus consumers are far worse off.

There are many examples where the privatization did not work as intended, but also numerous where the liberalization process was successful. With this example only a tendency can be perceived but not the general probabilistic outcome as too many factors of the environment and the circumstances have to be (re)considered.[12]

Summarized however it can be definitely emphasized that privatization processes are entry points of corruption, inefficiencies and exploitation.

---

[11] Source: Slocum, Tyson: “The Failure of Electricity Deregulation: History, Status and Needed Reforms”, Public Citizen´s Energy Program (2007) Pg. 7

[12] Fortelny, Marc-Joël: “When and how is regulation circumvented in the energy market?”, University of Vienna (2013), Pg. 4-5

2. The Effects of Corruption

Before an analysis of the topic's combination of corruption and the energy sector may be performed, it is absolutely crucial to first examine each of those individually. Examples though include the "cohesive partner" as well.

2.1 Definition Area of Corruption

The term corruption in an economic environment is defined as fraud, bribery, immorality and misuse of power. An example for a definition is the following of the business dictionary:

> *"Wrongdoing on the part of an authority or powerful party through means that are illegitimate, immoral, or incompatible with ethical standards. Corruption often results from patronage and is associated with bribery.* [13]

Various similar descriptions are used when outlining corruption often without considering the echoes and different ways of impact - the incentive of corruptive behavior on the side of the authorities are on the one hand assurance of maintaining that position and on the other hand gaining benefits for "distributing" this power. Generally speaking, the first result of such actions is a reduction of the (total) social welfare. However, this is not a short term and not even necessarily a monetary problem as such patterns are highly likely to induce a spiral. As a matter of fact, sufficient and preferably adaptive counter-measures are necessary to intervene and limit such actions.

The exact classification of the area of corruption is rather difficult as such arrangements may occur randomly in different sectors and transits may occur to the energy sector indirectly and become unidentifiable. Cases where bribery was involved in a monopoly concession auction are quite common, nevertheless mostly unknown to the public.[14]

---

[13] http://www.businessdictionary.com/definition/corruption.html (last accessed on 16.06.2013)

[14] http://www.europarl.europa.eu/document/activities/cont/201206/20120626ATT47717/20120626ATT47717EN.pdf (last accessed on 16.06.2013)

The probability that the corruptive behavior of only one local politician affects the energy sector on a huge scale is quite low but surprisingly possible (examples in the cases later on).

In this sector disruptive patterns are generated by conglomerates' lobbies, collusive partners in industries and politics, councils and greater political institutions (like the European Parliament or the House of Senate).

Another more deceiving part of manipulation is the desire to misinform and misinterpret "data". Not every technology reaches its predicted heights or wasn't even able to, in the first place in its current state of evolution (for instance debates about potential of wind farms).[15]

In the following chapters examples will determine how corruption shatters technology capabilities, waste energy, gamble in the financial markets etc.

2.2 Measurement of Corruption

The determination of corruption levels will be expressed and explained in the chapter of "The geographical Analysis" via the Corruption Perception Index (CPI).

The organization of "transparency" explored and researched the corruption of public sectors worldwide since 1996 while at the same time providing not only the results of their data but the process of collecting data, the weighing methods and the interpretation of this data as well.

As the characteristic of corruption is to deceive and hide its true nature this logically results in difficulties to measure it.[16]

---

[15] http://www.health24.com/Lifestyle/Environmental-health/News/Wind-farm-potential-overestimated-20130227 (last accessed on 16.06.2013)

[16] http://transparency.org/whoweare/history (last accessed on 16.06.2013)

As an example the inflation of potatoes in Central Europe originated in Germany from the three biggest "competitors". In collusion they achieved a price increase of over 40%.

Interestingly, this was the second highest price increase and has been proven to be corrupted while the number one good (onions) seems not to have been discovered or researched.[17] In this case, measuring corruption would be either an estimation based on statistics (similar to a statistic correlated to drug use of professional athletes) or an investigation where in- and outputs have to be recalculated which is a difficult and, depending on the scale and frequency, very costly method.[18]

Summarized, it can be said that statistical data indicates possible corruption and with sufficient data, may even define a more refined area of corruption.

2.3 Area of Impact

The effects of corruption are wide spread in the energy sector due to various factors. Not only is this sector (disputable) the most important economic base factor but also paradoxically a technology based "technology enabler".

Therefore irregularities produce technology setbacks (decrease of research speed), a reduction of businesses' growth (California case closure), carbon footprint (comparable to future costs that are shared globally) and also global turbulences of financial markets.[19]

As there are numerous scientific specializations of economics (for instance lean management, sustainability, cost-benefit analysis etc.) corruption itself is not in-between.

---

[17] http://www.focus.de/finanzen/news/verfahren-wegen-preisabsprachen-kartoffel-kartell-prellte-verbaucher-und-bauern-um-eine-milliarde-euro_aid_986263.html (last accessed on 16.06.2013)

[18] http://live.worldbank.org/monitoring-results-performance-indicators-enforcement-anticorruption-laws (last accessed on 16.06.2013)

[19] http://jia.sipa.columbia.edu/russia%E2%80%99s-financial-crisis-economic-setbacks-and-policy-responses (last accessed on 16.06.2013)

Because it is mostly hidden and not/or difficult to measure, depict and express even if there is a hub of research for corruption (transparency.org) a specialization has not been established in the studies of economics resulting in a "lack of" research compared to other topics.

Inevitably, the area of effect is indirectly noticeable in every technologically driven village, city or society as there are no "substitutes" for energy (compared to food). As a matter of fact, the area of impact is global.

3. Role of Regulation and its Methods

The most prominent factor of the theory of regulation is the choice and adaptation of a suitable method. While each of these methods have their strengths and weaknesses their correct and persistent implementation is the key to success in creating the most beneficial outcome for the social welfare.

This however will be just a short review of some of the methods as the more problematic part of corruption is the environment, the circumstances, the risks and the opportunities of regulation methods. Often the strict observance of efficient methods is already the first obstacle and/or collapse of the system.

When a firm naturally aims for profit maximization a control board has to be set against an unfavorable position of the consumers/ society. The task of setting an optimal regulation which leaves the financial capabilities and flexibility intact, while at the same time ensuring quality and a "fair" price, is comparable to Sisyphos, due its nature of the persistent struggle of enforcing a continuous work.[20]

3.1 Rate of Return Regulation – ROR

This type of regulation focuses on maintaining the characteristics and especially the advantages of a competitive market in a monopolistic one. The goal is that firms are allowed to make profits, but only up to a certain rate.
They can manage their input into the company on their own, the resulting output or the price to which they want to sell, as long as the revenues do not exceed the pre-established level of return. [21]

---

[20] Fortelny, Marc-Joël: "When and how is regulation circumvented in the energy market?", University of Vienna (2013), Pg. 6

[21] Brauetigam, Roland; Panzar, John: „Effects of the Change from Rate-of-Return to Price-Cap Regulation" American Economic Association (1993) The American Economic Review Vol. 83, No. 2, Papers and Proceedings of the Hundred and Fifth Annual Meeting of the American Economic Association, Pg. 191

This is a much-criticized model. The first ones that put this under scrutiny were Harvey Averch and Leland Johnson who declared in 1962 that a company trying to maximize its profits under these conditions would fail to minimize its costs.

In contract to an unregulated company, that would strive to use both capital and labor efficiently, a firm conducted under the rate-of-return restriction would employ too much capital at the expense of labor.
This is called the “Averch Johnson Effect”. [22] [23]

3.2 Revenue Cap

The choice of the revenue cap over the price cap normally induces a fixed or known quantity.

The limitation of the total revenue received by the firm to a certain sum in a time frame can be circumvented through implicit decisions on the actual rates or return on capital that is in employed with the intention to reach for the price limit edge. As a result it is often indistinctive to the ROR.[24] [25]

3.3 Incentive Regulation

As different regulation methods were implemented, that were not always advantageous for the companies' financial developments, an urge arose to create something that would bring gains.

---

[22] Viscusi, W. Kip; Harrington, Joseph E. Jr; Vernon, John M.: „Economics of Regulation and Antitrust“, MIT Press (1995) Fourth Edition, Pg.433-436

[23] Fortelny, Marc-Joël: “When and how is regulation circumvented in the energy market?”, University of Vienna (2013), Pg. 6-7

[24]http://regulationbodyofknowledge.org/price-level-regulation/features-of-price-cap-and-revenue-cap-regulation/ (last accessed on 22.02.2013)

[25] Fortelny, Marc-Joël: “When and how is regulation circumvented in the energy market?”, University of Vienna (2013), Pg. 7

The following three types of governance were specifically designed to motivate firms in introducing efficient cost – benefit processes, to be innovative and to improve quality.[26] [27]

3.3.1 Price Cap

As the name states, this type of regulation implies setting an upper limit for the prices firms are allowed to charge. It is a formula that subtracts the expected efficiency savings (X – average value based on the past performance of companies of the same sector) from the Consumer Price Index (CPI) thus attempting to reach the level of the overall rate of inflation of the economy.

As the savings are fixed, this method is supposed to create an opportunity for companies to maximize their revenues and pass the surplus to their shareholders.[28]

3.3.2 Yardstick Regulation – Benchmarking

Historical data has always proven to be very significant for studying purposes in any business sector. Naturally, this is also used as a method of regulation. Statistical, past information is gathered and with the support of specific mathematical models, the data can be analyzed and structured in such a manner that benchmarks can be set and even future events predicted.

The selection of the appropriate data and the underlying model is of utmost importance because misinterpretation can lead to significant losses.

For regulating purposes, five types of metrics are differentiated and put in practice. The Core Overall Performance Indicators relate on information available to the general public, such as output per employee, usual key performance indicators as ROACE, ROI, revenues.

---

[26] Viscusi, W. Kip; Harrington, Joseph E. Jr; Vernon, John M.: „Economics of Regulation and Antitrust", Fourth Edition, Pg. 436

[27] Fortelny, Marc-Joël: "When and how is regulation circumvented in the energy market?", University of Vienna (2013), Pg. 7

[28] Fortelny, Marc-Joël: "When and how is regulation circumvented in the energy market?", University of Vienna (2013), Pg. 8

These financial criteria fail to identify relations between the different factors, reason why regulators often chose to ground their studies on Performance Scores based on Production and Cost Estimates that highlight the best and worst performers out of a group.
The Virtual Company Approach tries to set a baseline for measuring performance, but it faces the challenge of distorted company information and the Process Benchmarking Concept that focuses more on management concerns rather than economic outcome.[29]
The last one is the Customer Survey Benchmarking that is on the one hand constructive, because it depictures the current view of the customers, but is highly inconclusive because the consumers can be easily manipulated and therefore little concrete payoff can be gathered.[30]

3.3.3 Earnings Sharing

Also called profit sharing or sliding scale regulation, this is another form of government that involves, as the name states, sharing of gains between the company and its consumers.
Of course, the regulated firm is allowed to keep its earnings as long as they do not exceed a pre-established rate of return.
Should this happen, the excess revenue will be returned to the customers, either through the means of direct payments or by lowering the prices. Nevertheless, should the firm generate much too low profits; these losses will also be shared with the consumers, generally by increasing the prices of the products.[31]

---

[29] Fortelny, Marc-Joël: "When and how is regulation circumvented in the energy market?", University of Vienna (2013), Pg. 8

[30] http://regulationbodyofknowledge.org/price-level-regulation/properties-of-benchmarking-and-yardstick-regulation/ (last accessed on 22.02.2013)

[31] http://warrington.ufl.edu/centers/purc/purcdocs/papers/0213_sappington_price_regulation_and.pdf (last accessed on 22.02.2013) , Pg. 3-4

4. General Structure of Energy Markets

The total structure of energy markets is worthy of a separate research due to its complexity. This chapter is a mere focus of points of interest and requires additional literature to fully understand the inter-connectivity, relations and interdependencies.

4.1 Outline of the U.S Market

The following info graphics depict the U.S. energy market in relation to the efficiency of usage, energy potential and certain indications of trends (which have to be interpreted).

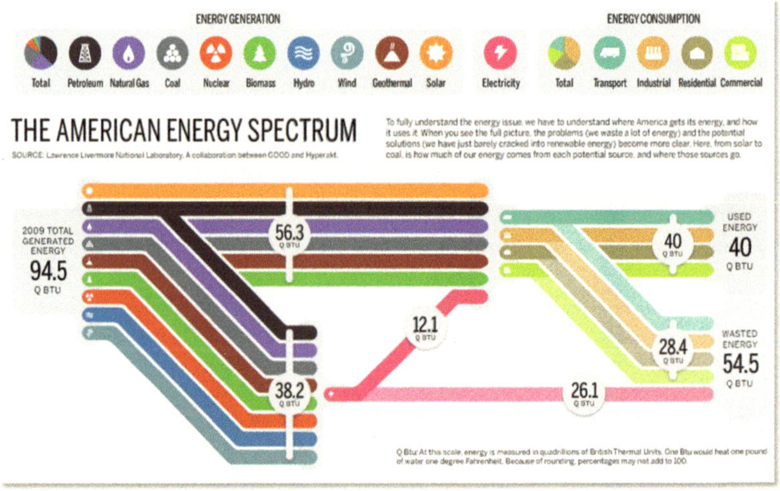

Figure 1: U.S Energy Spectrum [32]

First of all, the agreed term of BTU is rather confusing to the rest of the world which is using the metric system; nevertheless this unit remains sufficient if it is used persistently in comparison: a BTU (British Thermal Unit) is defined as the energy used or the potential used to heat one pound of water one degree Fahrenheit.

The energy levels shown below are stated in quadrillion BTUs.

---

[32] http://visual.ly/american-energy-spectrum?view=true (last accessed on 24.02.2013)

The U.S. market shows a rather great inefficiency regarding the level of wasted energy, which is approximately 60%. As a side remark, the term "American energy spectrum" is incorrect as it is in fact referred to the United States, which is a common mistake in the terminology of U.S. Americans.

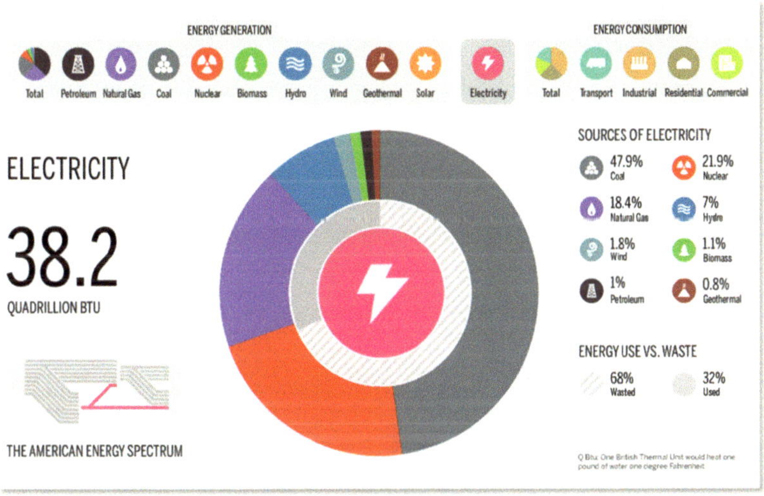

Figure 2: U.S Electricity Sector [33]

The U.S. electricity sector shows the effects of massive lobbying (which has always been strongly developed in the U.S. history) as the dependence of finite resources is at a very high percentage of nearly 90% which cannot be defined as "sustainable" considering future transitions.

The 22% of the nuclear sector depends on finite resources but in a completely different level regarding the classification of the energy potential compared to its mass.

Fossil resources have an "expiration date" due to their heavy dependence world-wide and are doomed to extinct in decades or centuries according to various calculations which differ greatly due to contrasting use of methods, estimations and approximations (see chapter 7 "Extracted Key Factors").

---

[33] http://visual.ly/american-energy-spectrum?view=true (last accessed on 24.02.2013)

The arguable part in this constellation is if corruption does actually occur or not despite obvious indications of irregularities (depending on the viewpoint). An argument against this would be that those finite resources have been proven to be the most cost and energy efficient possibilities. The high level of waste, namely 70%, is generated by the over usage of finite resources.

Another necessary statement is the clarification of the (nearly) total absence of solar power (See "Extracted Key Factors"). Surprisingly the announcement of increasing growth of several hundred percent is in fact a barely measurable amount compared to the total usage of other sources which is explained by the poor base level.

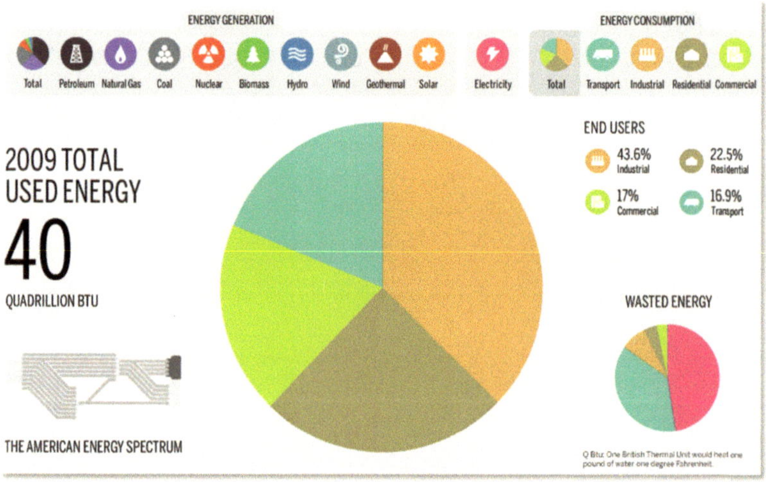

Figure 3: U.S. Total Used Energy [34]

The diagram above shows the percentage of the end users (namely 43.6% industrial, 22.5% residential, 17% commercial and 16.9% transport) and points out as well that electricity and transport contribute over three quarters to the total wasted energy levels.

It has to be noted that there is a strong interdependency of end users, when for example a good has been produced in the industrial sector, is then transported to a residential end user which then has steady energy consumption with it. Therefore the indirect contributions are not that transparent.

[34] http://visual.ly/american-energy-spectrum?view=true (last accessed on 24.02.2013)

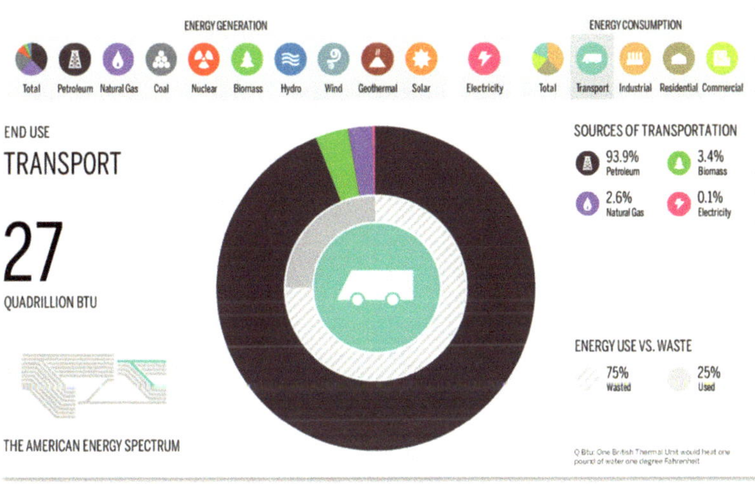

Figure 4: U.S. Use of Energy in Transport [35]

Aside from the high "wasted" level, the percentage of electricity is only at a remarkable level of 0.1% which indicates on the one hand the significance of ship and air transportation and the automobile industry but also a certain insignificance of railway transportation and the electric motors (see "Extracted Key Factors").

4.2 Outline of the EU Market

The European Energy market is quite different to the U.S. market in two major aspects which are the policies and the goals.

The European directives and policies are developed in a totally different mindset. The European government has acknowledged (officially) the finiteness of resources/ capacities and the necessity for sustainability. The following graphic pictures a collaboration for more energy efficiency in Central Europe which is based on a rather small investment budget but high potential for a better energy use with the already existing institutions, networks and sources in contradiction to the U.S. energy market which tends to "only" render new accessible sources.

[35] http://visual.ly/american-energy-spectrum?view=true (last accessed on 24.02.2013)

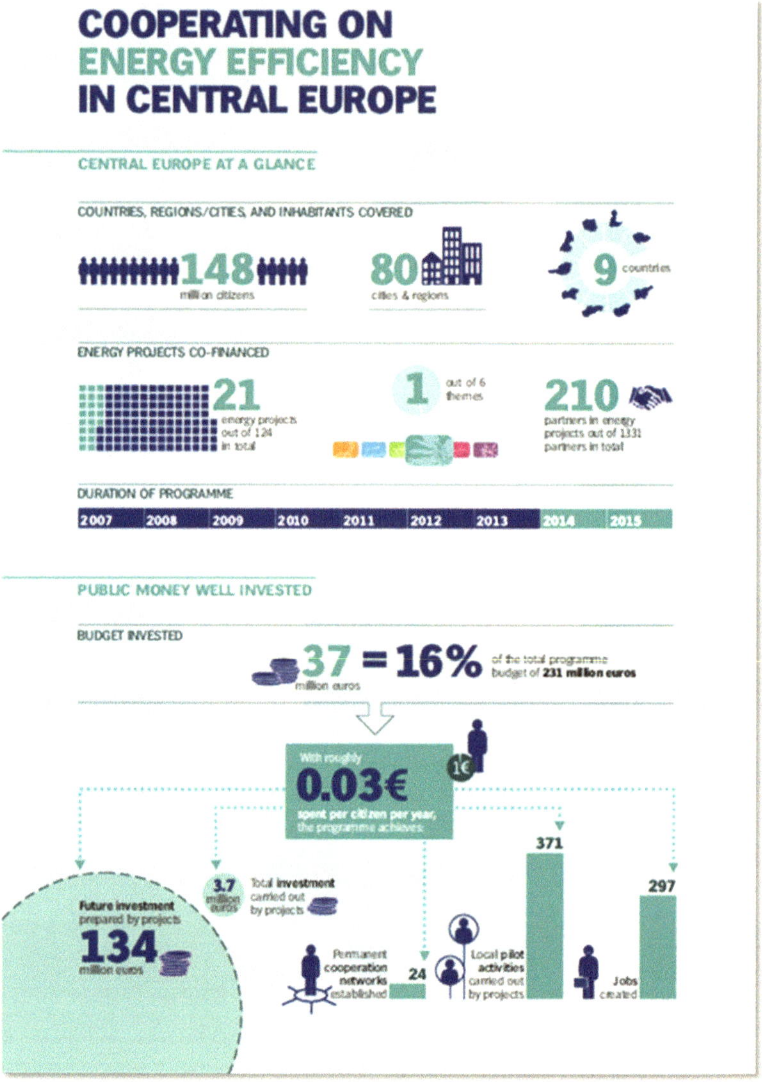

Figure 5: Europe Energy Efficiency Part I [36]

Additionally, those energy projects are co-financed, therefore less risk prone and in correspondence with regulation "smart investments".

[36] http://www.central2013.eu/typo3temp/pics/003eca7911.jpg (last accessed on 15.06.2013)

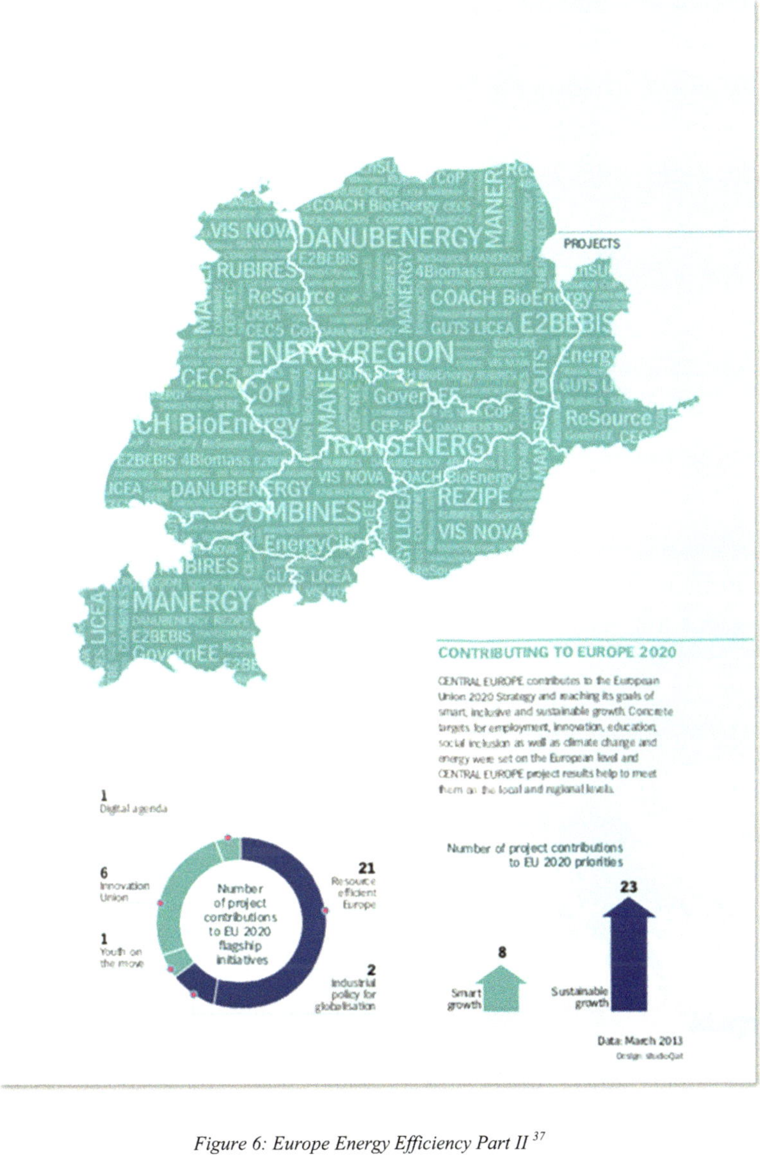

Figure 6: Europe Energy Efficiency Part II [37]

The more noteworthy part of the outline of the European energy market is the power shift regarding the share of energy from renewable sources.

---

[37] http://www.central2013.eu/typo3temp/pics/003eca7911.jpg (last accessed on 15.06.2013)

The following graphics contradict statements such as “renewable energy is not as efficient…”, “renewables are far more costly”, etc.

Before further investigating this transition it has to be noted that the corruption part in this matter is the misinformation of actual energy possibilities on both sides, namely the under- and overestimation (which will be further discussed in “Extracted Key Factors”).

In the long run energy production has to be made out of renewable sources without the aspect of nuclear power potential. The problem of this framework is that energy demand has a certain fluctuation and renewable energy production has very distinguishable characteristics, such as weather –affection, accessibility and transferability (see “Extracted Key Factors”).

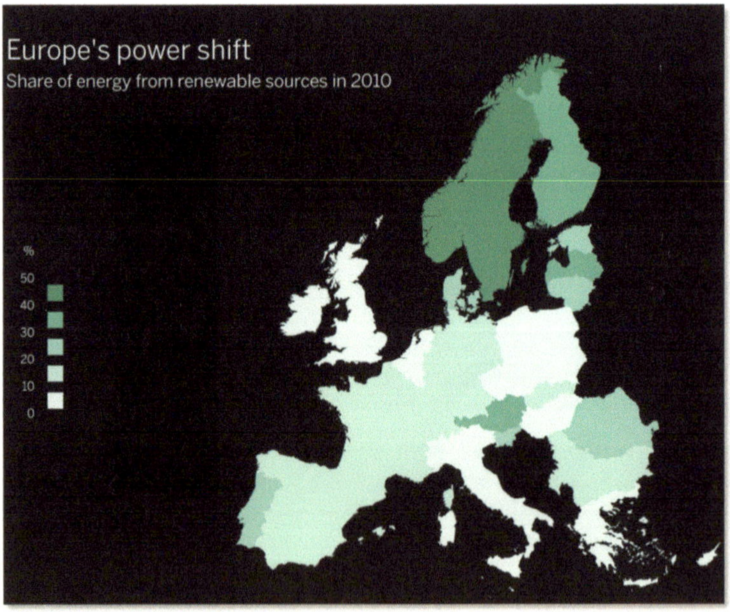

Figure 7: Europe's Power Shift [38]

---

[38] http://visual.ly/europes-power-shift (last accessed on 15.06.2013)

Every European country agreed to increase their renewable energy production percentage level according to their capabilities. When the different levels of 2009 and 2010 are analyzed, the aspect of total energy production has to be considered as the percentage is compared to the total amount.[39]

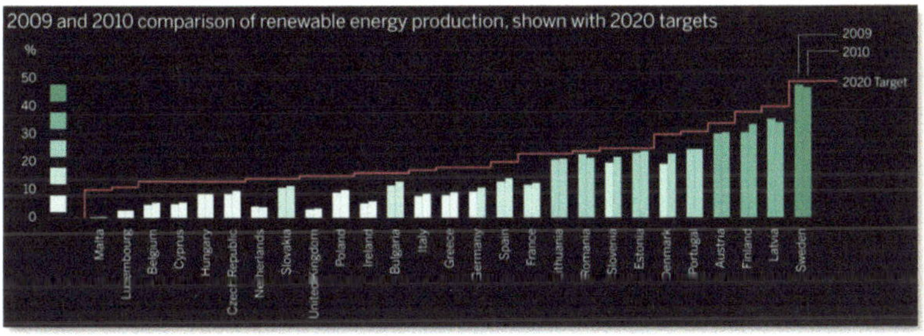

Figure 8: Percentage Change in Renewables [40]

A rough approximation of the graph below indicates that countries with a higher (20 and above) percentage of renewable energy have set lower growth goals, which may correspond to the knowledge of their possibilities. If a country wants to double or triple etc. their percentage level in a mere decade, the likeliness of success is low as historical examples in various sectors and time frames have shown.

An overall transition (according to figure 9) can be identified as the shift from oil and petroleum, solid fuels and nuclear sources to gas and renewables has taken place which is and was also induced by European directives.

Major changes in the energy mix and therefore in the infrastructure and market itself cannot be performed in small (too small) timeframes due to a lot of factors particularly the increase in gas is explained by the European government as the stability factor for providing a steady production when the more fluctuating renewables are increased.

---

[39] http://blueandgreentomorrow.com/features/infographic-renewable-energy-in-europe/ (last accessed on 15.06.2013)

[40] http://visual.ly/europes-power-shift (last accessed on 15.06.2013)

The shaping of a public opinion (that gas is more or less also classified as a clean source like renewables) is scientifically seen confusing but politically seen explicable. This can be defined as a compromise as the transition to renewables is not yet possible without a stable energy production based on a finite source.

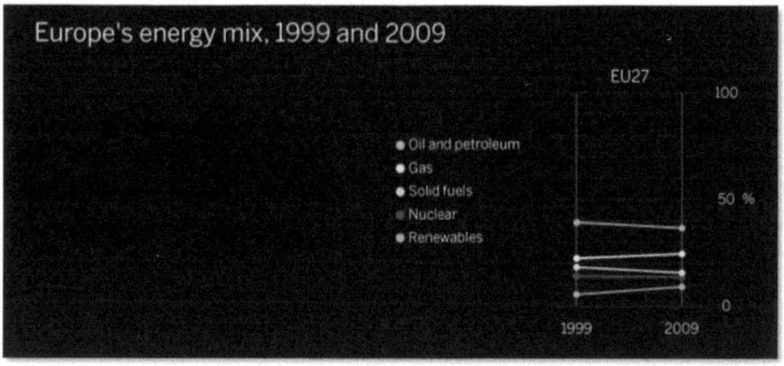

Figure 9: Europe's energy mix (1999-2009) [41]

In figure 10 tendencies of an increase in renewables overall can be identified where Austria and Denmark have the greatest increase in a renewable percentage and a decline in the rest of the sources.

However, Denmark had the steepest rise in renewables due to the rather low starting position. Interestingly, Cyprus with an extremely high percentage in oil and petroleum indicates a strong dependence and an inflexibility to change.

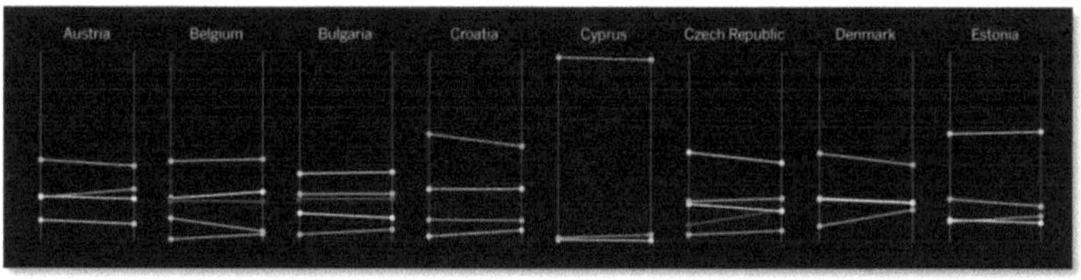

Figure 10: Europe's energy mix Austria to Estonia (1999-2009) [42]

---

[41] http://visual.ly/europes-power-shift (last accessed on 15.06.2013)

[42] http://visual.ly/europes-power-shift (last accessed on 15.06.2013)

Ireland and Italy are the examples for fossil fuel swap of oil and petroleum to gas transition with a very small percentage change of renewables. Some of the countries are just more or less stable in their energy demand and production like Finland, for instance.

France is one of the few countries which had an increase in oil and petroleum, while at the same time showing an extreme reliance on the nuclear energy sector. An overall increase in gas power is identifiable with only a few exceptions (Hungary).

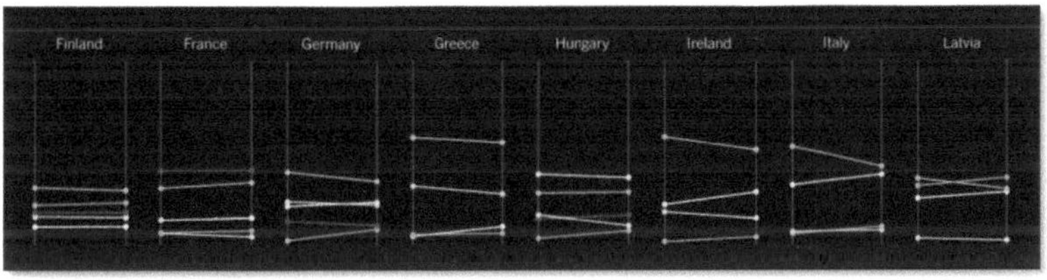

Figure 11: Europe´s energy mix Finland to Latvia (1999-2009) [43]

Malta is very similar to Cyprus considering the lack of variety which resembles purposely on the lack of investment. Norway shows a high level of renewables but also an increase in oil and petroleum which is logical when facing an abundance of resources.

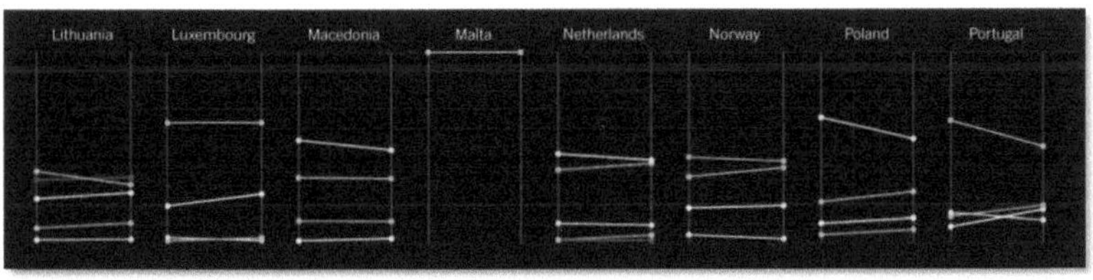

Figure 12: Europe´s energy mix Lithuania to Portugal (1999-2009) [44]

---

[43] http://visual.ly/europes-power-shift (last accessed on 15.06.2013)

[44] http://visual.ly/europes-power-shift (last accessed on 15.06.2013)

Turkey's unique position, geographically seen, is too compelling to not overinvest into gas energy production which explains the shift of the only increase and the greatest decrease in the renewable percentage of all countries (one of the few decreases in general).

Sweden has faced a certain barrier in efficiency with enlarging the renewable portfolio while reducing their nuclear and oil petroleum levels and trying to stabilize the market with a steady growth of smart grids and high yield renewable projects (smart investments).

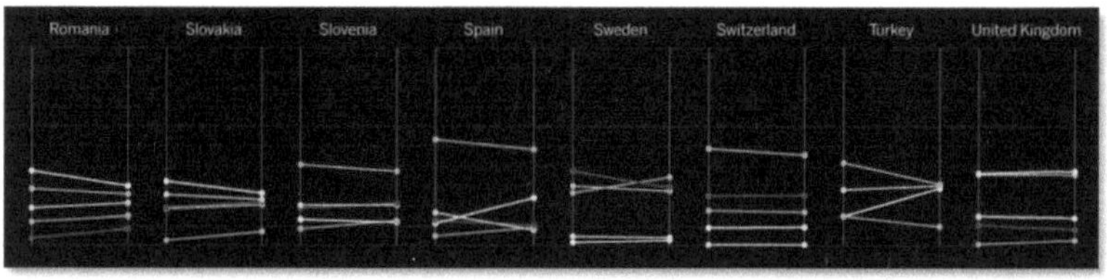

Figure 13: Europe's energy mix Romania to U.K. (1999-2009) [45]

The general trend of increasing the renewables' percentage was induced by subsidies from new projects in their construction and in their energy price. While the countries increased mostly the renewables, they often balanced it with an increase in gas which is propagated as the cleanest solution of the fossil fuels.

[45] http://visual.ly/europes-power-shift (last accessed on 15.06.2013)

5. Geographical Analysis of Significant Factors

This section deals with a combination of research knowledge regarding general corruption in the public sector and more or less specific corruption in the energy sector.

The goal of this comparison is to identify a correlation or a tendency of coherency between them. The main source of scientific papers is the organization of Transparency which has a unique way to identify, indicate, measure, evaluate and repel corruption. These tests are differentiated by nationality and internationality.

5.1 Analysis of the Corruption Perception Index (CPI)

Before analyzing the methods and results of the CPI (Corruption Perception Index) the history of transparency.org is worthwhile. In 1993 Peter Eigen, a retired World Bank official, founded together with nine allies the small organization now widely known as Transparency International in Berlin.[46]

In the early nineties corruption in development projects was usual and a so-called "taboo" topic. The main inspiration for the foundation was Eigen's experience in East Africa. In the following years global recognition, corruption as an input for the world agenda, law changes for foreign bribery (made by the OECD) and many more changes were achieved.[47]

The two most influential publications were the so-called CPI and the TI Source Book (TI stands for Transparency International) which has been issued the first time in 1995, while the CPI is issued annually. As the approval and the respect of the anti-corruption movement has risen, the funding and the participation enabled greater amounts of data, surveys, research in general and also other methods, like the Bribe Payer's Index (BPI), various reports etc. to be published.[48]

---

[46] http://transparency.org/whoweare/history (last accessed on 15.06.2013)

[47] http://transparency.org/whoweare/history (last accessed on 15.06.2013)

[48] http://transparency.org/research (last accessed on 15.06.2013)

The CPI is described by TI as followed:

> *"The CPI scores and ranks countries/territories based on how corrupt a country's public sector is perceived to be. It is a composite index, a combination of surveys and assessments of corruption, collected by a variety of reputable institutions. The CPI is the most widely used indicator of corruption worldwide."* [49]

So in fact the CPI only resembles the perception of business people and country experts in a range of a pre-determined way to capture the levels of corruption. Each country has to have at least three different sources for building a CPI. In 2012 nearly all of the countries were evaluated except those in white (in the graphic below). The performance points from 0 to 100 indicate the measurement from highly corrupt to very clean. In the beginning only a few countries participated with much less material/data.

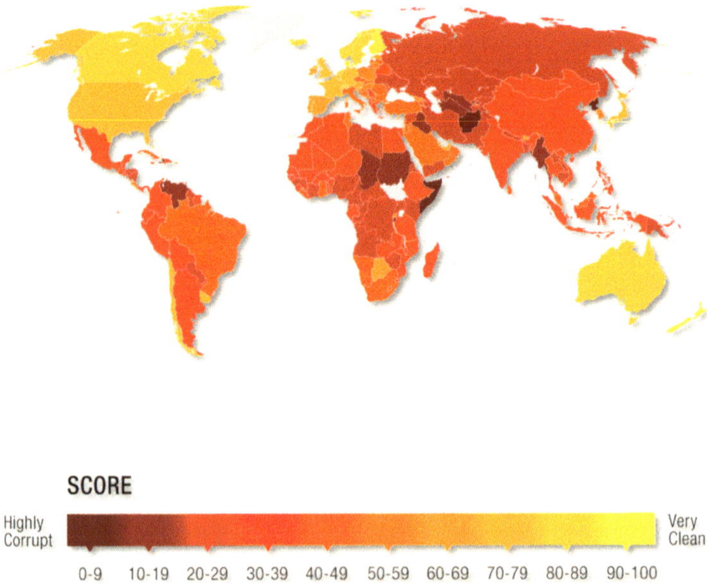

Figure 14: Global Map of the CPI [50]

---

[49] http://cpi.transparency.org/cpi2012/in_detail/ (last accessed on 15.06.2013)

[50] http://cpi.transparency.org/cpi2012/ (last accessed on 15.06.2013)

The main concern of this chapter is to determine if a tendency of the CPI is coherent with the performance of the energy sector. This comparison is experimental, because both analyses are based on a mere perception or trend. The reason for this is the nature of corruption which has been explained before. Therefore absolute levels of corruption are not achievable and have to be simulated via statistical estimations. (For further details the link http://files.transparency.org/content/download/534/2217/file/JRC_Statistical_Assessment_CPI2012_FINAL.pdf) Additionally, every other research aspect is fully available in detail on the transparency.org hub.
Furthermore, it has to be stated that public scandals through the media influence affects the CPI rather strongly.

5.2 Correlation of the CPI and the respective Energy Sector Performance

The first country examined is Russia with a rank of 133 (out of 174 rated countries) and a score of 28 (measured by CPI).[51] The exact reasoning for this score would be too complex to discuss in detail (or every other country).
However, the current state of Russia regarding its democracy level, the presence of bribery (further discussed in the following sub-chapter), a history of corruption (transition from communism to capitalism) and a lack of corruption penalties (in number and amount) with several recent scandals such as the Hydro Power scandal[52] are sufficient reasons. The energy sector of Russia is quite consistent; the performance of this sector is relative coherent with the CPI considering the inefficiencies of distribution and production of energy (also caused by resource abundance). The overall performance improves when only revenue is evaluated and huge losses caused by corruption are ignored. A lack of future investments and smart grids, renewables (sustainable energy) and so forth, round up a rather negative perception of Russia. Anti-corruption movements have started already, but before they can be successful on a bigger scale the mindset has to change regarding efficiency (wasting).

[51] http://cpi.transparency.org/cpi2012/results/ (last accessed on 15.06.2013)

[52] http://rt.com/politics/scandal-corruption-putin-energy-488/ (last accessed on 15.06.2013)

India is a more difficult example with a rank of 94 and a score of 36,[53] but a far worse operating energy sector when the focus lies upon the electricity part. With the recent massive power shortages and instabilities of the grid, a mismanagement of this particular part of the energy sector is obvious even if according to study of KPMG the energy sector is perceived to be as the least corrupted sector, study which has been published before the last scandals.

Therefore the perception has likely shifted as well. This example is so difficult to explain in short as the history of India and its energy sector is and was heavily influenced not by market mechanisms but by political decisions. The misinvestments of Enron[54], for instance, still take its toll on the energy supply. It is arguable how great the influence of corruption is on the energy sector, but its involvement is undeniable and in this particular case, has even been prognosed beforehand.

As a side remark, it has to be stated that shortages of a real good become far quicker apparent than, for example financial inefficiencies.

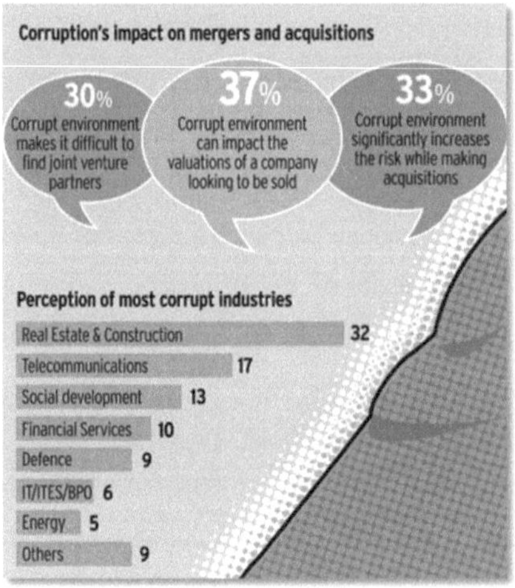

Figure 15: The Cost of Corruption in India – KPMG Part I [55]

---

[53] http://cpi.transparency.org/cpi2012/results/ (last accessed on 15.06.2013)

[54] http://www.igidr.ac.in/faculty/nag/FDI%20in%20India%20in%20the%201990s.pdf (last accessed on 15.06.2013)

[55] http://visual.ly/cost-corruption (last accessed on 15.06.2013)

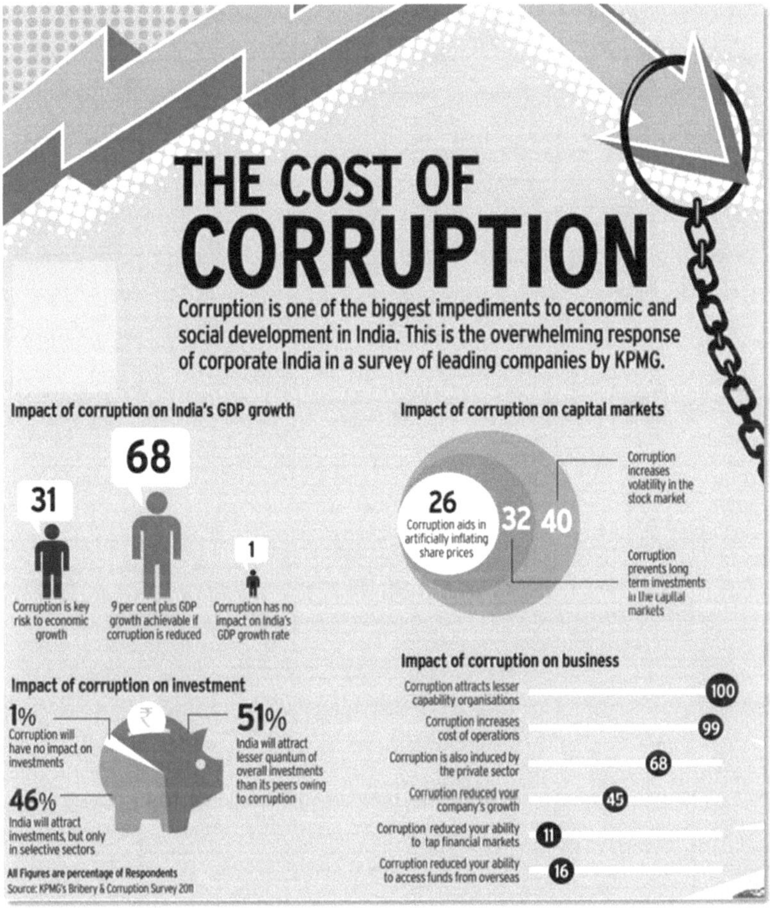

Figure 16: The Cost of Corruption in India – KPMG Part II [56]

Denmark is the perfect example for a nearly corruption free nation that pursues persistently its future goals. Compared to other nations, it was free of scandals and the performance of the energy sector has been measured as very efficient. Denmark has also a very promising energy mix towards renewables (percentage- wise the greatest increase – as shown before in chapter 3.2). Denmark is ranked as number 1 and scored a CPI of 90.[57]

---

[56] http://visual.ly/cost-corruption (last accessed on 15.06.2013)

[57] http://cpi.transparency.org/cpi2012/results/ (last accessed on 15.06.2013)

The case of Austria is however different, where various political influences lead to a steep increase in corruption in the public sector mostly directly correlated to economic relationships between politicians (high ranked) and the leaders of companies.

Those scandals have blunt names like “Telekom scandal”, “Buwog scandal” etc. where large monetary flows have been hidden (with so called tax payer’s money) to benefit a few, who hazarded the consequences of public losses.

The rank of Austria is 25 with a score of 69 and the perception of the energy sector is much more similar to Denmark regarding efficiency and the energy mix. As a result it can be said, that perception is obviously always partly subjective. [58]

The opposite example is the U.S. with a rank of 19 and a score of 73, however relativized a rather poor performing energy market regarding efficiency, energy mix and price regulation is predominating (as shown in chapter 1.4 and 4.1). [59]

However, it cannot directly be compared to the inconsistent performance of Russia as losses were generated mostly by speculation and on purpose falsely calculated investments (as it will be shown in chapter 6.1).

The differentiated state of performance and corruption can only be expressed in tendencies and not in mere numbers, therefore the U.S. has a negative tendency in the energy sector performance and a positive tendency (only perceived in the general public sector).

As the size in the CPI is statistically normalized, the U.S. is the opposite example of Austria considering the upwards and downwards tendencies of scandals.

---

[58] http://cpi.transparency.org/cpi2012/results/ (last accessed on 15.06.2013)

[59] http://cpi.transparency.org/cpi2012/results/ (last accessed on 15.06.2013)

5.3 Bribe Payer's Index 2011

This report is particularly interesting, as it ranks 28 of the world's largest economies in measuring a probability of its companies to pay bribes abroad. This unique overview provides insights of the correlation between the firm's integrity in the home country and abroad. It is also noteworthy that since the last BPI in 2008 there has been on average no improvement.[60]

The energy sector is affected when public contracts, such as the construction of new power plants or new grids or a monopoly concession auction in involved. Indonesia has to be pointed out for numerous private contracts and a respective listing of number 25 of 28 listed countries.

The last two countries have a great impact on the global energy sector due to their importance, namely China and Russia. China's efforts to combat bribery lack in enforcement as legislation changes and greater penalties have to actually be carried out. Before 1st May 2011 the Chinese law did not even consider extraterritorial elements. In short, a lack of regulation provided the opportunity for corruption.[61]

The Vice Chair of the Anti-Corruption and Governance Research Center Transparency International China, Ren Jianmin declared the following:

> *"The new amendment of the penal code marks the Chinese authority's commitment to combating corruption. However, there are tremendous challenges ahead and bottlenecks that need to be cleared. Not only does the appropriate legislation need to be put in place, but effective implementation of this provision also requires sufficient enforcement processes and resources, international cooperation and moreover, the continued willingness of the authorities to treat this issue as an important priority."* [62]

---

[60] Hardoon, Deborah; Heinrich, Finn: "Bribe Payers Index 2011", Transparency International (2011), Pg. 15

[61] Hardoon, Deborah; Heinrich, Finn: "Bribe Payers Index 2011", Transparency International (2011), Pg. 15

[62] Hardoon, Deborah; Heinrich, Finn: "Bribe Payers Index 2011", Transparency International (2011), Pg. 15

Russia also passed a new legislation in May 2011 that criminalizes foreign bribery with penalties for companies and individuals. An improvement will be shown only over time.

Elena Panfilova, the Director of the Center for Anti-Corruption Research and Initiative Transparency International Russia, stated:

> *"The position of Russian business in the 2011 Bribe Payers Index is not of any surprise since Russia in general is still struggling to find the proper way to confront systemic corruption. It would be strange to expect business to do better than public office does. Unfortunately, as far as the spread of corruption is concerned, there are no islands of integrity in Russian public and business life. But there is hope that the strict enforcement of new national anti-corruption legislation and compliance with international commitments will help to change this situation in the coming years."* [63]

As shown in the following table, the legitimacy of the energy sector abroad performs far worse in matters of bribery and therefore corruption. Power generation and transmission combined with oil and gas are at the lower end of the ranks (13 and 16 out of a total of 19 countries). This proves instability in behavior patterns in the energy sector.
Especially small bribery transactions are far more common abroad to speed up bureaucratic processes or to enable construction projects in the first place. Certain parts of the energy sector are hazardous to the environment and costly in the long run – to avoid those costs bribery is used again (explained in chapter 6.3).

---

[63] Hardoon, Deborah; Heinrich, Finn: "Bribe Payers Index 2011", Transparency International (2011), Pg. 15

RANK	SECTOR	SCORE	NUMBER OF OBSERVATIONS	STANDARD DEVIATION	90% CONFIDENCE INTERVAL	
					LOWER BOUND	UPPER BOUND
1	Agriculture	7.1	270	2.6	6.8	7.4
1	Light manufacturing	7.1	652	2.4	7.0	7.3
3	Civilian aerospace	7.0	89	2.7	6.6	7.5
3	Information technology	7.0	677	2.5	6.8	7.1
5	Banking and finance	6.9	1409	2.7	6.8	7.0
5	Forestry	6.9	91	2.4	6.5	7.3
7	Consumer services	6.8	860	2.5	6.7	6.9
8	Telecommunications	6.7	529	2.6	6.5	6.9
8	Transportation and storage	6.7	717	2.6	6.5	6.9
10	Arms, defence and military	6.6	102	2.9	6.1	7.1
10	Fisheries	6.6	82	3.0	6.0	7.1
12	Heavy manufacturing	6.5	647	2.6	6.4	6.7
13	Pharmaceutical and healthcare	6.4	391	2.7	6.2	6.6
13	Power generation and transmission	6.4	303	2.8	6.1	6.6
15	Mining	6.3	154	2.7	5.9	6.6
16	Oil and gas	6.2	328	2.8	6.0	6.5
17	Real estate, property, legal and business services	6.1	674	2.8	5.9	6.3
17	Utilities	6.1	400	2.9	5.9	6.3
19	Public works contracts and construction	5.3	576	2.7	5.1	5.5
	Average	6.6				

Table 2: Perceptions of foreign bribery by sector [64]

6. Case Studies of Corruption and Counter-Measures

In a complex world case studies with simplified models and highly specified solutions are a mere prelude to the insights that can and have to be achieved with a supranational anti-corruption agenda (as described in 8.2).

Actually the counter-measures and their success heavily rely upon the cause of the corruption ex ante. It is sometimes difficult to determine the root of the cause – is the origin regional, national or even supranational? Further explained by the chapter 7 "Extracted Key Factors" the most severe forms in fact originate supra-national and have therefore to be addressed accordingly.

---

[64] Hardoon, Deborah; Heinrich, Finn: "Bribe Payers Index 2011", Transparency International (2011), Pg. 15

6.1 Speculation and Artificial Shortages – Case of California

The crisis of California is one of the most outrageous examples of failed regulation, corruption throughout the energy and financial sector and the hazardous combination of financial methods without a matched limitation.

A modification or a readjustment is mostly possible in a minor or mediocre problem case. Enron however induced a breakdown of not only of the energy cycle, but many different institutes, funds and workforce.

Huge sums of assets have just been vaporized. After analyzing the case itself a closer view on Enron might reveal the correlation of corruption and the attitude of apathy combined with an overly emphasized opinion of deregulation. [65]

6.1.1 History in a nutshell

California was one of the most regulated energy markets in the U.S. before the deregulation process has started in 1996.

The government of the state has started to slowly modify the controls in the sector intentionally to increase competition. The most memorable date was September 23rd 1996 when the Electric Utility Restructuring Act (Assembly Bill 1890) was enforced. Soon after in 1998 the spot market for energy has started (electricity and gas). [66]

At the start of the collapse the state of California factually had a capacity of 45 GW but during the blackouts the demand was significantly lower. Through the evaluation of recorded tapes of the traders it has been revealed that various schemes have been applied and enforced by them.

---

[65] Fortelny, Marc-Joël: "When and how is regulation circumvented in the energy market?", University of Vienna (2013), Pg. 13

[66] http://www.ferc.gov/industries/electric/indus-act/wec/chron/chronology.pdf (last accessed on 22.02.2013)

The first stage was to sell huge amounts of "yet abundant" energy outside of the country at a moderate or even low price. They held the exceeded capacity outside with other power plants and then proceeded with the second stage when they artificially shut down various power plants in California for maintenance, checkup etc. As the demand grew without limitation of the now scarce resource, it was not possible for the regulatory mechanism to apply to the whole sale market – in fact only the retail sale market could be regulated by law enforcement and the distribution companies had no choice but to pass on the high costs.

As a result, not only blackouts occurred but throughout the business sectors huge losses or even foreclosures took place. The end of the California crisis – disregarding its aftermath – was also the downfall of Enron that exceeded its core business so far beyond every regulation that a collapse of the overinvested, bound or lost capital was inevitable.[67]

The dispute of "who to blame" as various media have discussed is still ongoing. Most scientists (and journalists) are convinced that a combination of a lack of regulatory authority and the reckless over-risky behavior of Enron has led to this disaster. But not without several participants in the market whether it be banks, politicians and personnel from the power plants who knew that certain actions of Enron could not be justified.[68]

6.1.2 Enron – ask why.

The history of Enron is too huge to unravel it completely but some of the highlights (mostly in a negative way) were pointed out across this analysis.
Beginning with the highly corruptible way of their accounting (mark to market) which they preserved with hiding losses (investing in Nigerian oil tankers for a

---

[67] http://www.ferc.gov/industries/electric/indus-act/wec/enron/summary-findings.pdf(last accessed on 22.02.2013)

[68] Fortelny, Marc-Joël: "When and how is regulation circumvented in the energy market?", University of Vienna (2013), Pg. 13-14

period of six months) and creating artificial future earnings they "did not hold back" according to media.
These future earnings were often far off the probability scenario (the Blockbuster case has only made losses yet Enron has created a cash flow line for the next 20 years without waiting for the first year to finish).
Initially, a distributer and provider of natural gas and an innovator of energy trades (as widely seen as a positive financial innovation) the visions and ideas of Enron came too far off every possibility to have a sustainability which is a key factor in the energy sector.

Lastly said, too shorten the complex accounting books scheme, the financial fraud "attacks" and so forth it must be stated that Enron was so unregulated that it became not only a danger to itself, its closer environment, but to the global stability (also linked with the "dot com" bubble)[69].[70]

6.2 Theft of Power – Case of Turkey

Rather recent changes in the structure of the electricity (energy) market have enabled new possibilities and opportunities for factual restructuring and modernizing the energy policies. The question is if this progress can or cannot be achieved judging by the history so far. The regulatory agency that should supervise this process and the implementation is the Energy Market Regulatory Agency or "EMRA".
The Republic of Turkey Prime Ministry Privatization Administration or shortly only called "PA" has initiated the privatization of Turkey's core electricity distribution utility, Türkiye Elektrik Dağıtım Anonim Şirketi – in short "TEDAS". TEDAS and its distribution companies are Turkish State-owned joint-stock companies conducting business in the distribution and retail sale of electricity and provision of retail services to the end-consumers. "With approximately 28 million customers, 93 billion kWh of electricity sales and 98% market share in electricity

---

[69] Fox, Loren: "Enron: The Rise and Fall" John Wiley&Sons (2003), Pg. 211

[70] Fortelny, Marc-Joël: "When and how is regulation circumvented in the energy market?", University of Vienna (2013), Pg. 14

distribution across Turkey in 2005, TEDAS and its distribution companies together form one of the largest organizations in the country." [71]

Privatization of distribution companies are executed by using a Transfer of Operating Rights ("TOR") backed Share Sale model ("TSS model").[72]

Based on this structure an investor is the exclusive owner of the distribution company´s shares, which is the unique licensee for the allocation of electricity in the determined region. He does however not have the ownership of the distribution network assets and other items that are essential for the operation of these distribution assets.

The true ownership of these distribution assets will stay in control of TEDAS and only indirect possession can be achieved by the investor. Via his shares he has the right to operate the distribution assets facing to a TOR Agreement with TEDAS.[73]

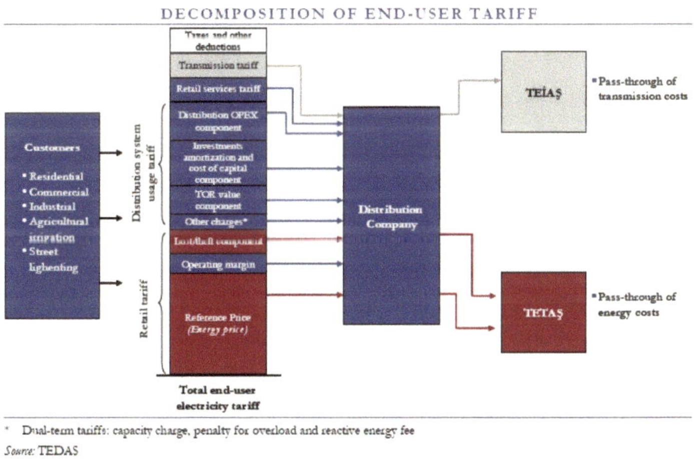

Figure 17: Turkish Electricity Tariff Schemata [74]

---

[71] http://www.oib.gov.tr/tedas/teaser_english.pdf (last accessed on 22.02.2013) Pg. 1

[72] http://www.oib.gov.tr/tedas/teaser_english.pdf (last accessed on 22.02.2013) Pg. 3

[73] http://www.oib.gov.tr/tedas/teaser_english.pdf Pg. 1 (last accessed on 22.02.2013)

[74] Source: Türkiye Elektrik Dağıtım A. Ş.in cooperation with Lazard – Tedas Privatization Teaser, Pg. 4

As it can be seen in the figure above, the dual-term tariff is rather complex and sophisticated yet well and modern applied. The privatization process of the various entities of the electricity (energy) market has been executed rather slowly and according to the laws of the regulatory framework.

The State-Owned status still remains within these structures to a certain extent and provide more control than a full (and quick) liberalization. Interesting is the dual cap of revenue and retail price.

The revenue caps are expected to be *guaranteed* regardless of the consumption levels in the region. Given that a distribution company undercuts its revenue cap due to lower usage, tariff adjustment is allowed for the following time frame under the rule and surveillance of EMRA.

Furthermore the approved revenue caps for 2006-2010 have been revised due to inflation, based on the changes in the Electricity Market Index ("EMI") as announced by EMRA before the occurrence (which indicates an adaptive and responsive institute with a strategic plan).

Additionally, the distribution company may reflect any changes in its energy wholesale reference costs to the price cap through a pass-through mechanism under the surveillance of EMRA.

So far so good – are there any major regulation issues? Turkey seems to pursue willingly to adapt modern state infrastructures and controlling using a lot of knowledge of the experience of other systems. The question is where "the catch" might be.

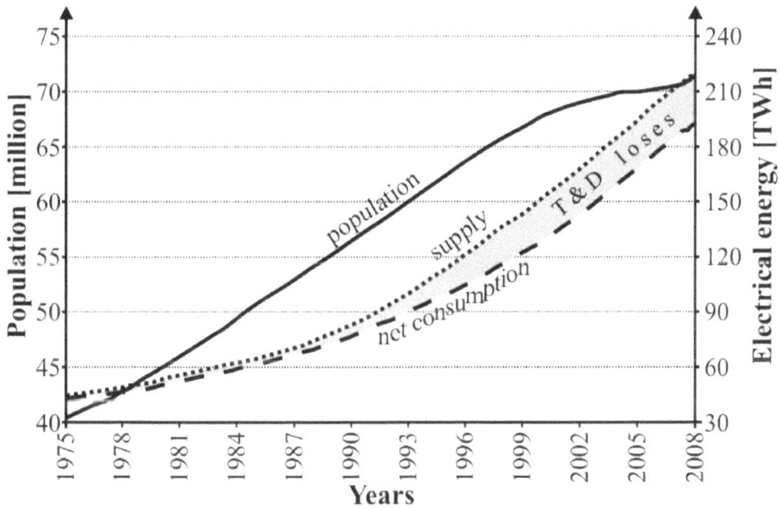

Figure 18: Turkish Electricity Theft Graph [75]

Transmission and Distribution or T&D losses are normally in the low one digit area or even beneath it. In fact in Europe those losses are problems of the grid, oversupply that has to be outsourced without trading and so forth. In Turkey however these losses are mostly theft on an industrial and professional level.

Until now Turkey lacks so called "smart grids" which would analyze the connections and could report imbalances at the end points. In the current state losses are perceived but cannot identified on a closer level without spending huge sums (smart grid investment – law enforcement etc.).

As a result those losses in theft are on the rise and are actually greater than these depicted on the graph as it was an estimation from mid-2000 onwards.

> *"Despite all efforts, the rate of electricity theft in Turkey increased from 14.4 percent to 17.7 percent from 2008 to 2009, recent data from the Turkish Electricity Distribution Company (TEDAŞ) has shown."* [76]

---

[75] Source: Türkiye Elektrik Dağıtım A. Ş. – http://www.tedas.gov.tr/Sayfalar/Anasayfa.aspx (last accessed on 22.02.2013)

[76] http://www.todayszaman.com/newsDetail_getNewsById.action?load=detay&link=218239 (last accessed on 22.02.2013)

This is a public secret and the tendency is upwards and not downwards as the government does not act suitably. Politically this seems to be ignored as the poverty of certain regions hinders a liberal approach of equalization. Not only is the theft of electricity dangerous, it vaporizes value with on-going long-term effects of disinvestment.

Momentarily the government pays the distribution companies (private operators who bought a monopoly concession) their loss. An effect that is similar to the mechanism of subsidy, which is debatable as well (see 7.1).

Therefore Turkey is a suitable example for good regulation mechanisms lacking one major aspect and therefore struggling with balancing on a Sisyphos basis (readjustments done quarterly).[77]

6.3 Integrity loss by Alienation – Case of Argentina, Nigeria etc.

Electricity companies and oil/gas companies (chiefly from Chile and the United States) constitute almost all foreign investment in Argentine power generation.[78] While foreign investments, involvements and contributions are not exceptional in a modern global economy a quotation by *Paracelsus (1493-1541)* indicates the precarious matter:

> *"Poison is in everything, and no thing is without poison. The dosage makes it either a poison or a remedy."*

This quotation does not only apply to this particular topic but to many. It is arguable depending on the situation and performance of the foreign firms if a huge percentage of foreign shares are either good for growth and prosperity or perhaps malicious for control and social benefits of the (home) country.

---

[77] Fortelny, Marc-Joël: "When and how is regulation circumvented in the energy market?", University of Vienna (2013), Pg. 15-18

[78] http://online.wsj.com/article/SB10001424052702304432704577347801235907294.html (last accessed on 22.02.2013)

It cannot be denied that (regardless of pro or contra national beliefs) there is a certain interference of various factors if the regulatory board consists of persons of the home country and the foreign firm mostly or completely of foreign people.

There are possible language barriers, cultural habits/ behavior and many differences overall which retard every process of agreement, readjustment etc.

The point is - simply put – that alienation is a controversial factor which is hard to determine.[79]

Whereas Argentina deals with price problems and interest conflicts in their energy politics the oil spillage in the Niger Delta is increasing in damages and costs. The foreign part-investor Shell has failed to oppose corruption and is facing and has faced several law suits, while declaring innocence.

> *"Criminal activities and abuse of the pipelines were the main causes in which they never participated" (according to Shell).*

The costs of the removal of the oil waste are estimated in the billions with a timeframe of 30 years. The question remains if in total the actions produced more benefits than costs, which is calculated differently depending on the opinion of the researcher.

> *"Shell is one of the largest companies in the Netherlands, a country jealous of its image as an environmentally friendly beacon to the world. But the company's problems in Africa serve as a reminder that even the Dutch get some of their energy from fossil fuels that are extracted from poor countries under ambiguous circumstances."*[80]

---

[79] Fortelny, Marc-Joël: "When and how is regulation circumvented in the energy market?", University of Vienna (2013), Pg. 18

[80] http://www.nytimes.com/2013/01/31/business/global/dutch-court-rules-shell-partly-responsible-for-nigerian-spills.html?pagewanted=all&_r=0 (last accessed on 16.06.2013)

6.4 Cash Flow Redirection – Case of Ukraine

In the late 1990´s the chaos in the wholesale electricity market of Ukraine could be perceived by the crash of the funds administration. The distribution between the generators and the service providers was supposed to be proportionally to the factual revenues that were gained by selling electricity at certain price and volume. The actual outcome was that service providers got the short end of the stick as they could not collect fully from the users and therefore were not paid in proportion.

Hence an algorithm was created for distributing the available funds according to the relative sales of the service providers. That was the idea in theory – in practice the result aberrated. This a perfect example of a fitting method with a corrupted and unstable environment which prevents the correct application.

The Ministry of Fuel and Energy, or Minenergo[81], disturbed the equilibrium several times by detouring cash flows to chosen (preferred) providers, covered by the argument that it was an emergency payment.

The rules implied that if a distributor has not completely paid for the energy resources he bought, he will be excluded from future interchange.

Nevertheless Minenergo flawed the algorithm again by not enforcing this rule framework and instead tried to address the problem by fabricating new agreements with central and local governments on customers that could be disconnected without political repercussions.

Of course some of the distributors took advantage of the negligence of payment obligations and obviously withheld money that has already been collected from their customers of the market.

---

[81] http://siteresources.worldbank.org/INTENERGY2/Resources/electricitsourcebookch8.pdf (last accessed on 22.02.2013) Pg. 93

The exceedance of negotiations and other noncash payment modes (mutual cancellation of payment obligations, promissory notes, and tax write-offs) even further eroded the preservation of the regulatory framework for the market of the Ukraine.

Non-cash transactions provided huge tax advantages as the cash that was received in an company's bank account was mostly seized. On the other hand those non-cash payments had limited fungibility and the market operator could only distribute cash payments.

After a while collections dipped below 80 percent, of which the share of non-cash transactions in the power industry has exceeded 80 percent - the economy wide average was about 40 percent - and cash payments dropped below 10 percent - non-payments accounted for this balance. To only cash that actually was used belonged to the paying population and therefore a growing imbalance was created.[82]

Most of the generators and their respective fuel suppliers received miniscule parts of the monetary pool. Ironically even the funds that were issued to the distributors – by the (not upheld) algorithm - did not cover the costs of the networks and the customer services.

Finally it can be said that the structures behind the methods are crucial for a functioning market and that willingness to maximize profits is not a guarantee by far that the "invisible hand" regulates and balances the market. In that case a downward spiral led to disaster and proceeding losses of society and the firms.[83]

---

[82] http://siteresources.worldbank.org/INTENERGY2/Resources/electricitsourcebookch8.pdf (last accessed on 22.02.2013) Pg. 93

[83] Fortelny, Marc-Joël: "When and how is regulation circumvented in the energy market?", University of Vienna (2013), Pg. 19-20

7. Extracted Key Factors

This crucial part of the research is a collection of the filtered knowledge of cases, correlations, explanations and clarifications. An endless list of cases would not reflect sufficiently/efficiently the essence of corruption which is defined not always by the circumstances but rather by the opportunities.

The strict definition of corruption does not provide insights of its weighs and methods that in fact do not always include monetary transactions or a disruptive behavior.

Several parts of these extracted key factors consider the way information is provided and interpreted. Scientifically seen, the most dangerous circumstances are those in which an adapted methodology, scientifically approved methods, objectivity and innovation are neglected due to misinformation (propaganda), falsified data and lobbying (corrupting).

7.1 Subsidies and Social Welfare

There are certain methods and mechanisms in the energy (or public) sector that have to be critically supervised by a well-educated and experienced regulatory board.

As subsidies are perceived more in a negative than in a positive way from an economic perspective the long-term strategy should not rely upon heavy subsidies.

The argumentation that public goods and "necessities" have to be as cheap as possible to increase social welfare is more than controversial. A graph will follow in the next sub-chapter to depict the imbalance that occurs when applying subsidies.[84]

How can a subsidy in terms of an energy tariff prices look like and what is the outcome from the perspective on total social welfare?

---

[84] Fortelny, Marc-Joël: "When and how is regulation circumvented in the energy market?", University of Vienna (2013), Pg. 9-10

With a rather rudimentary non-elastic model certain aspects of a shifted supply curve can be depicted with an on-going new equilibrium and an increased consumption. In this example the subsidy is 10 € Eurocents or 0,1 € per unit – a kilowatt per hour.
The increase from 20 MW to 25 MW is the result of this consumption incentive.

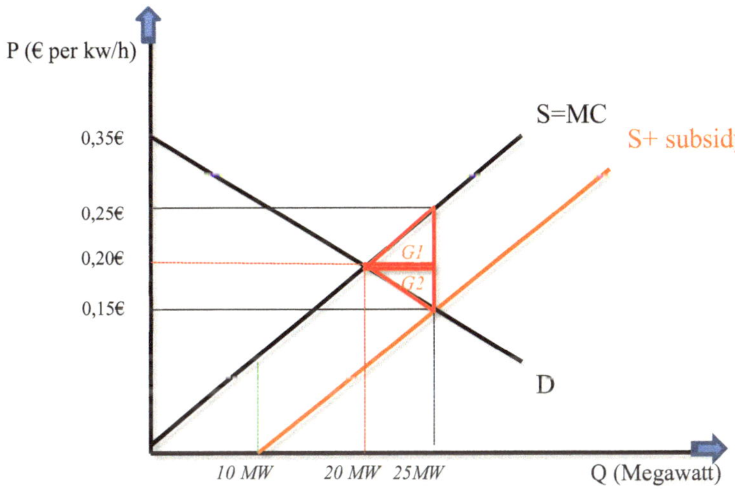

Figure 19: Graph of an energy-subsidy impact on social welfare [85]

A result from this "benefit" by the price reduction from 0,20 € to 0,15 € is that clients consume more but pay less and suppliers can provide more at a lower price. Disregarding the possible flexibility of supply and demand, the cost of the new equilibrium is defined by the sum of *G1* and *G2* which is the government spending induced by the subsidy.

The difference of the price at the consumption point for the producer and the price that has to be paid by the client is given by the government as 0,10€ per unit. 5 MW are consumed more now.
(0,1 * 5)/2 = 0,25   As 1 MW equals 1000KW the outcome is 0,25*1000 = 250€

---

[85] Source: Marc-Joël Fortelny

At first 250 € seems to be a bearable amount for this city. However this is the calculation for only an hour. Ignoring peak-load times with a simplified overall average usage of 25 MW per hour the loss in total social welfare in a year is
250€ *24*365 = *2 190 000 Euro*

Although this model and these calculations are only rudimentary the implication of a certain questionability of subsidies has to be acknowledged even with a consideration of various unprofitability factors in public sectors! [86]

Various subsidies are heavily criticized and still issued regardless of the profitability of the respective sector. In the case of the U.S. oil sector billions are granted. The following quotation questions the reasoning of a huge deduction.

> ***"The domestic manufacturing deduction for oil and natural gas companies ($11.6 billion):*** *In 2004, as American manufacturing was being ravaged by China's entrance on the global scene, Congress passed legislation designed to encourage companies to keep factories operating in the U.S. Thanks to some intensive lobbying, the oil industry ended up as one of the beneficiaries. But while the refining process does involve high-tech manufacturing, there was never any danger that either drilling or refining was going to migrate overseas."* [87]

Lobbying will shortly be discussed in chapter 7.5 to provide a certain insight to identify the thin border between lobbying and corrupting.

---

[86] Fortelny, Marc-Joël: "When and how is regulation circumvented in the energy market?", University of Vienna (2013), Pg. 10

[87] http://www.theatlantic.com/business/archive/2013/03/americas-most-obvious-tax-reform-idea-kill-the-oil-and-gas-subsidies/274121/ (last accessed on 16.06.2013)

7.2 Financial Innovations

As far as financial innovations may help the energy sector they also can be devastating to the sustainability of the energy market. If they help only short-term and fail long-term it can be defined as a double-edged sword, a tool that may lead to a disastrous outcome.[88]

Certain skepticism remains when financial products claim to solve "all" of the problems in a particular area of the energy sector. The most common part is financing projects, another is insuring a project and lastly to refinance current operations through capital transitions.

This is only a very basic classification considering the endless possibilities of combined and innovated financial methods. Whereas some products provide great benefits, doubtful financial providers of too exotic products should be avoided as the example of California has shown through Enron.[89]

7.2.1 Market Trade

Many methods have been already established in the energy market, from the standard oil trade, to the transition of MW or GW, to emission certificates and even shares of power plants are a standard connection to the financial market.

New financial innovations are difficult to rate without a certain period of testing and the resulting experience. One of these as an example is the speculation "how the wind blows" in terms of possible wind power generation and consistency in the article of Forbes journalist Tom Konrad in his article "Financial Innovation is Blowin′ in the Wind". [90]

---

[88] Fortelny, Marc-Joël: "When and how is regulation circumvented in the energy market?", University of Vienna (2013), Pg. 9

[89] Fortelny, Marc-Joël: "When and how is regulation circumvented in the energy market?", University of Vienna (2013), Pg. 11

[90] www.forbes.com/sites/tomkonrad/2011/05/24/financial-innovation-is-blowin-in-the-wind/ (last accessed on 22.02.2013)

Essentially the author implies that two innovations provide a new outcome of the wind market as investors who want to create a risk hedge fund regarding wind variability and secondly an option to buy a guarantee of a predetermined timeframe of new and existing maintenance contracts.

When financial matters overshadow the essential part of the energy sector, namely to produce and distribute efficiently energy to and for society, a certain questionability of the benefit in this case occurs.

Without any data sets a precarious observation might lead to future insights but so far no updates in that particular matter have occurred. The solution to the question can be the disclaimer of the author, which states that no investments should be done based on this article.[91]

7.2.2 Mark to Market – Accounting Methods

This hyper flexible method of accounting, which will be further discussed in context in the next chapter, is probably the most dubious accounting method that has been created.

To put it briefly, any future cash flows can be registered in the accounting books which are validated today and dividends or the value of shares are already handled today without the consideration of "fantasy trades". Mark to market became famous via Enron and its downfall. The corruption possibilities are numerous and the urge to manipulate the financial standing of the firm is also too great.

After the California crisis a ban of this method was demanded by many politicians, however it is still in use so far with the argumentation that the method itself is not corrupt. The advantages and disadvantages are highly disputed. As an example one perspective of the crash of the Californian market is that the regulatory board could not have certain insights and was therefore unable to regulate Enron successfully.

---

[91] Fortelny, Marc-Joël: "When and how is regulation circumvented in the energy market?", University of Vienna (2013), Pg. 11

Essentially the working paper states that the regulatory board is not the participant to blame due to the accounting method and the ways of conducting business by Enron.[92] [93]

7.2.3 Advancement into New Sectors

An approach to a new (and especially to an unknown) sector has to be done in a careful and thoughtful way. Additionally synergy effects, comparative knowledge and sufficient capital are key factors in success. The questionable examples of Enron regarding three financial innovations in new sectors, which had quite an impact are extraordinary.

For Instance the "Blockbuster" deal of Enron ended in a fraud on a high scale, where video on demand should have been provided via broadband[94], speculations about the weather did surpass Enron until today (the creation of derivatives is theoretically not limited by amount or issue)[95] and finally the so called "band width bloodbath" where Enron tried to trade with unused capacity of the broadband.[96]

It can be assumed, referring to these examples, that regulation in the energy sector cannot be performed properly if the firm is circumventing the range of action with the transition of capital towards such kind of investments which of course potentially ends in corruption. According to Deakin a focus in the core business is

[92] Deakin, Simon: "Learning from Enron" University of Cambridge (2003)Working Paper No 274, Pg. 13ff

[93] Fortelny, Marc-Joël: "When and how is regulation circumvented in the energy market?", University of Vienna (2013), Pg. 11-12

[94] http://www.justice.gov/opa/pr/2003/March/03_crm_153.htm (last accessed on 22.02.2013)

[95] http://caraellison.wordpress.com/2009/09/14/cnn-misrepresents-enrons-weather-futures/ (last accessed on 22.02.2013)

[96] http://www.wired.com/techbiz/media/news/2001/11/48732?currentPage=all (last accessed on 22.02.2013)

mandatory as the obligation of providing energy is very important to society and to the stability of the market.[97]

7.3 The Finiteness of Resources

To depict this matter in a mathematical (arithmetical) way, an analysis of a finite resource and how this scarce resource is commonly perceived is suitable. An example for a manipulative way of stating a situation is the report of the WCA (World Coal Association). The statements are contradicted by logic and syntax.

> *"It has been estimated that there are over 847 billion tonnes of proven coal reserves worldwide. This means that there is enough coal to last us around 118 years at current rates of production. In contrast, proven oil and gas reserves are equivalent to around 46 and 59 years at current production levels."*[98]

There are several questionable parts of this short quotation. First of all, the mixture of "estimated" and "proven" as a notation in the same sentence is an opposition. Secondly, it is misleading to use unreliable projections where the factors are confusing, in particular the rates of production at present and the production of the future.

Without scientific knowledge it could be understood that coal would last 118 years, which would induce a careless behavior, as this date is far in the future. To use the current production rates for the future while ignoring the necessary growth is misdirecting.

In this case 118 years of producing/consuming 847 billion tons of coal would mean about 7 billion tons per year.

After an assumption of 3% steady growth the number of years to last are halved at mere 51 years to exceed the reserves, though this is rather uncertain as it is

---

[97] Fortelny, Marc-Joël: "When and how is regulation circumvented in the energy market?", University of Vienna (2013), Pg. 12

[98] http://www.worldcoal.org/coal/where-is-coal-found/ (last accessed on 24.08.2012)

questionable if the production rates can be preserved and how much of the reserves (847 billion tons) actually exists and are effectively accessible.[99]

At the growth rate of 3 % (r) the doubling time would be:

Td = ln(2)/ln[(1 + (r/100)] = 100*ln(2)/r =69,315/3= 23,1 years ; it is rather precarious to have an increase in production like that.[100]

It is alarming if you exaggerate and extend this example to a steady growth of 10 % per year where only after 26 years the resource would be exhausted. To get to the heart of the matter the levels of production and consumption are more or less equal at the moment. However, as soon as the peak of production is reached, it is in fact not possible to maintain the level of production and therefore the consumption – incidental remark: the oil crisis of the seventies was such a case, where momentarily production could not satisfy the demand. It is common knowledge that the model for this is a Gauss bell curve. That is why technology that is too heavily dependent on finite resources cannot be seen as sustainable and therefore a continuous growth cannot be maintained.[101]

---

[99] Appendix 1 - a calculation sheet

[100] http://controlgrowth.org/double.htm cross reference of Dr. Bartlett (last accessed on 24.08.2012)

[101] Fortelny, Marc-Joël: „Unavowed aspects of the Financial Crisis and its aftermath / bottom (-) line“, University of Vienna (2012)

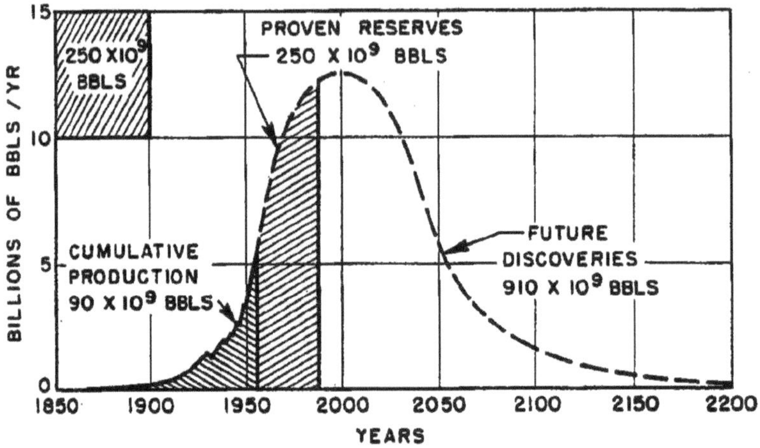

Figure 20 - Ultimate world crude-oil production based upon initial reserves of 1250 billion barrels.

Figure 20: World crude-oil production estimation [102]

> *"Peak oil is a real phenomenon and major objections to it do not hold up under closer examination. OPEC reserve figures are questionable and Saudi Arabia may not be able to produce as much oil as has been previously forecasted. Technology, though it will allow for more extraction of oil, will be unlikely to provide the substantial increases in oil supply that will be necessary to meet future demand because investment risks, underlying physical constraints, and production costs will likely remain too prohibitive. [...]Government restrictions, such as those present in the U.S., can place slight limits on oil production but they are immaterial factors in the global oil market. Abiotic oil, though an interesting concept, is a scientifically invalid theory as indicated by the fact that no significant quantities of abiotic oil have ever been discovered in the approximately 150 years of commercial oil production."* [103]

---

[102] http://www.geo.cornell.edu/eas/energy/_Media/mkh_oil.jpeg (last accessed on 16.06.2013)

[103] Ralston, Jonah J.: ""Peak Oil": The eventual end of the oil age", Washington University in St. Louis (2008), Doctoral Thesis Pg. 25

Essentially the peak oil theory emphasizes the fact that renewable energy is not an option to this point but an obligation due to the fact that oil production will decline and therefore cannot uphold the energy production at this rate. To round all off The following graphs show a comparison between finite and infinite resource production with today's technology considering *the amount of used resources.*

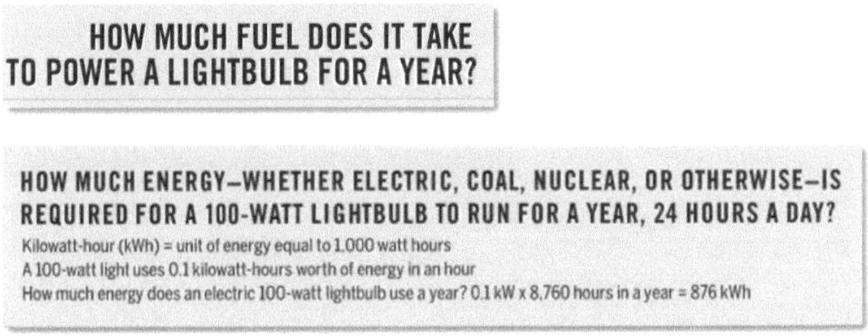

Figure 21: Energy Comparison [104]

[104] http://lindseynicholson.org/wp-content/uploads/2012/09/energy-comparison.jpg

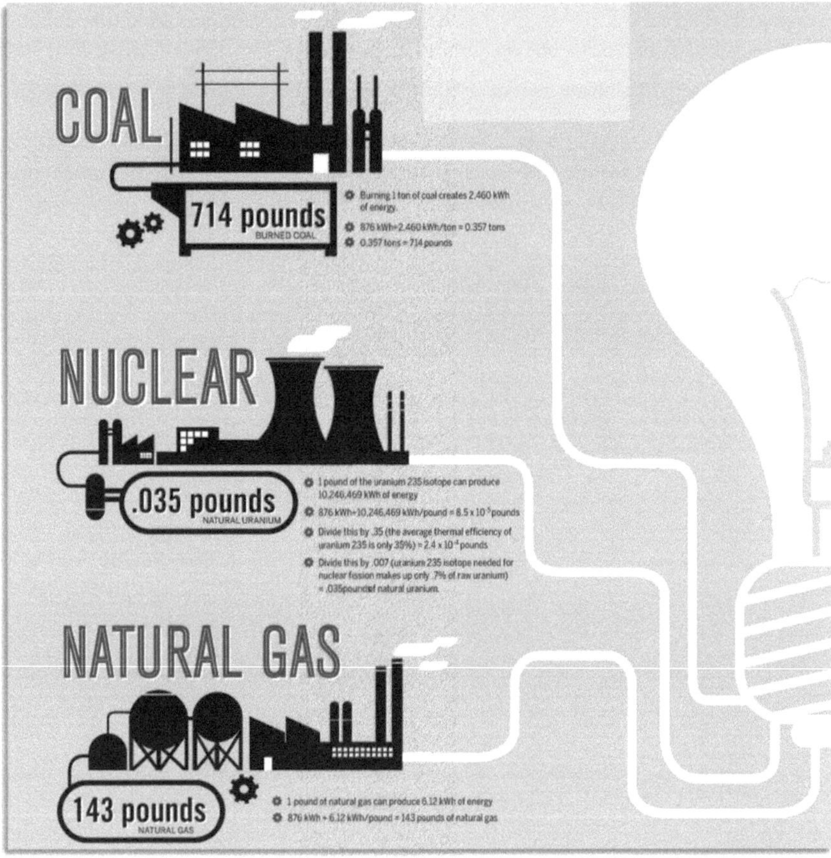

Figure 22: Energy Comparison Finite Resources [105]

[105] http://lindseynicholson.org/wp-content/uploads/2012/09/energy-comparison.jpg

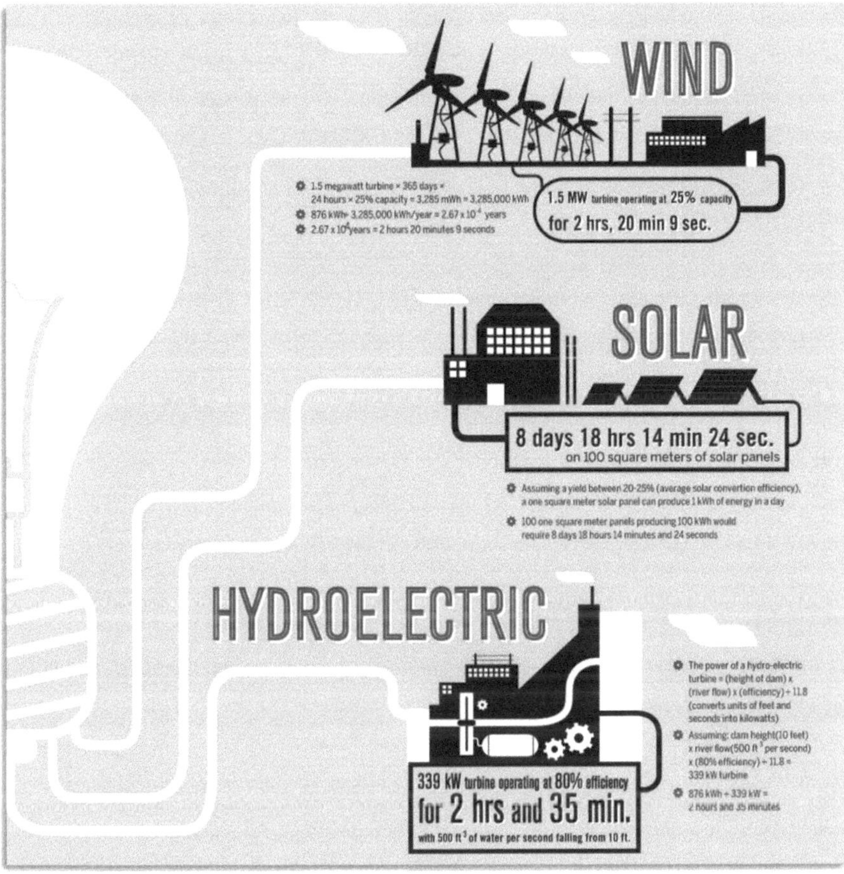

Figure 23: Energy Comparison Renewables [106]

7.4 Misinformation - Corruption of data

An undervalued part of corruption systems is the targeted misinformation of facts, relations, possibilities and opportunities. The most prominent factor here is a grade under- and overestimation of factors to empower a mostly lobbied opinion – a connection to finiteness of resources also is applicable.

[106] http://lindseynicholson.org/wp-content/uploads/2012/09/energy-comparison.jpg

As corruption works in secrecy the true purpose of suspicious actions are revealed commonly via a scandal (in general "when it's too late"). As a result, literature concerning corruption and the gathered knowledge and interpretation surfaces long after possible counter-measures and/or immediate actions is implemented. Consequently, pre-emptive regulations and actions have to be planned and consistently performed.

The debate over PV (photovoltaic), solar energy is scientifically disputable when various factors are weighted differently or even ignored (due to limitation, simplification or even lobbying).

The most commonly publicly perceived false fact is that solar energy is already used in "huge numbers". In chapter 4.1 the extremely small amount of 0.1 Q BTU (out of 94.5 Q BTU total energy mix) accounts for the yet unused potential.[107]

The graph on the next page shows the U.S. consumer perception and it's different to the reality. Furthermore, it depicts that the leader in solar energy, Germany, is by far more involved in the PV sector.

At the same time, considering chapter 3.2 Germany is one of the European countries with a rather low renewables percentage rate and subsequently a new question arises as to how tendencies of the PV sector are currently evolving and how strong.

[107] http://visual.ly/american-energy-spectrum?view=true (last accessed on 24.02.2013)

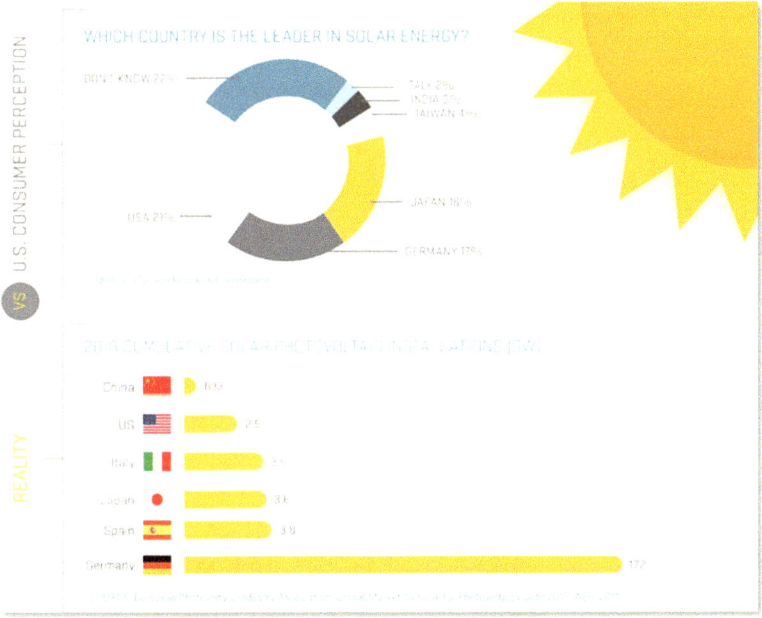

Figure 24: U.S. Consumer Perception of PV Rankings [108]

With the knowledge of the prior discussed facts the prognosis of the University of Toronto depicts an extremely overestimated energy mix share of solar energy, while subtracting the coal energy part completely. In 2011 the world energy portfolio consisted of a mere 11 % and in 2050 these estimations consider solar energy to be at 20 % in 2050 (while currently solar energy in 2011´s portfolio is not even recognizable).

The Shell Student Energy Challenge, an infographic competition, awarded this creation with the second place of all of the participants of America. [109] While different opinions naturally occur in debated topics, a discrepancy of this level should support such an overly idealistic paragon.

---

[108] http://www.appliedmaterials.com/sites/default/files/infographic_730w_1_0.jpg (last accessed on 15.06.2013)

[109] http://www.shell.com/global/environment-society/ecomarathon/events/americas/fan-zone/highlights/student-energy-challenge.html (last accessed on 16.06.2013)

Furthermore the yield level with the current technology and the resource expenditure is mostly not taken into account when dealing with the topic of PV.
PV cells need certain resources which are scarce again, like Indium and Germanium. Solar energy mass production on such a scale would lead directly into depletion or severe scarcity (economic costs rise). The provided article is one of many which indicates this problem. [110]

Figure 25: Global Energy Mix Transition Prognosis of the University of Toronto[111]

Additionally, detailed in chapter 4.2, even the current agenda of European goals is far off compared to this global prognosis – the aim is roughly a 20 % of renewables in total on average. While Europe accounts for 15% of the total global energy output, it is the Union with the most and highest ambitions regarding growth of renewables. In short it has to be pointed out that unscientifically approaches of future estimations distorts the perception and therefore corrupt.

---

[110] http://www.forbes.com/sites/energysource/2010/07/07/14-efficiency-for-thin-film-solar-cells-but-where-will-the-indium-come-from/ (last accessed 16.06.2013)

[111] http://www.greatenergychallengeblog.com/2013/06/06/student-infographic-contest-paints-bright-picture-of-youth-concern-on-energy-and-climate/ (last accessed 16.06.2013)

7.5 Lobbying as a Destabilizer

The total sum that was spent via lobbyists (2188) for the sector of energy and natural resources accounted for $379,789,053 according to the Senate of Public Records – dark figure is unnoted. A certain questionability has to be raised.

Industry	Total spending
Electric Utilities	$145,483,813
Oil & Gas	$140,143,996
Misc Energy	$48,570,147
Mining	$32,316,168
Environmental Svcs/Equipment	$5,881,939
Waste Management	$5,072,575
Fisheries & Wildlife	$2,320,415

Table 3: Lobby Spending in U.S. in 2012 [112]

The definition of lobbying resembles in some aspects the term of corruption:

> *"The act of attempting to influence business and government leaders to create legislation or conduct an activity that will help a particular organization."*[113]

Conferring to U.S. law lobbying is perceived as a petition to achieve goals which is rather difficult to separate from bribery (corruption). [114]

A consistency in the approach and the addressing of this issue a huge undertaking as the system is deeply implemented in all profitable sectors. Lobbyists of renewables rallied for their causes as well and achieved growing subsidies for the energy production which is applied to the electricity price for example similar to 7.1 with the negligence that without the subsidies a considerable part of the investments lose their profitability after the time span of support.

---

[112] http://www.opensecrets.org/lobby/indus.php?id=E (last accessed on 16.06.2013)

[113] http://www.businessdictionary.com/definition/lobbying.html (last accessed on 16.06.2013)

[114] http://www.renewableenergyworld.com/rea/news/article/2010/12/top-25-u-s-energy-lobbyists-of-2010 (last accessed on 16.06.2013)

8. Application of Counter-Measures

When the "Extracted Key Factors" are understood and its resulting insights are applied correctly and consistently supranational an upwards tendency regarding anti-corruption processes can be identified when the legislation and its enforcement is adapted comparing the (slow) conversion of the CPI.

The following last two subchapters are focusing on the example of a showcase model and the general application and maintenance of counter-measures. The U.K. Bribery Act is a recent considerable change in corruption perception by a government which is applicable to other nations and therefore has supranational prospects. Corruption has to be fought not only in the home country but also abroad – consequently this leads to a necessity of border crossing solutions.

8.1 The U.K. Bribery Act as a showcase model

The UK Bribery Act (entered into force 2010) enables a new approach for dealing with bribery abroad and enlarging jurisdictional reach.[115] Generally the law and its purpose can described in short as followed:

> *"The new Act is very broad in scope, capturing both bribery within the private sector and bribes paid to overseas government officials. Its jurisdictional reach is also very long, allowing almost no hiding place for companies which for some misguided reason decide to pay bribes.*
>
> *While the public consciousness of good corporate governance is forever improving and becoming more demanding and many companies are raising their anti-bribery standards, it is a sad truth that there is no sign that bribery in its many forms is decreasing."*[116]

---

[115] Wilkinson, Peter: "The 2010 UK Bribery Act Adequate Procedures", Transparency International (2010), Pg.4

[116] Wilkinson, Peter: "The 2010 UK Bribery Act Adequate Procedures", Transparency International (2010), Pg.1

Including four prime offences, adaptations were made to meet the requirements of the 1997 OECD Convention on Combating Bribery of Foreign Public Officials in International Business Transactions:

> *"Two general offences covering the offering, promising or giving of an advantage, and requesting, agreeing to receive or accepting of an advantage;*
> *A discrete offence of bribery of a foreign public official; and*
> *A new offence of failure by a commercial organization to prevent a bribe being paid to obtain or retain business or a business advantage (should an offence be committed, it will be a defense that the organization has adequate procedures in place to prevent bribery)."* [117]

Coherently penalties were raised with the option to fine individuals as well with imprisonment as an adequate consequence for severe cases. The guide of the U.K. Bribery Act that is quoted provides practical examples to identify smaller and greater issues. A classical case study is that of "planning gain related to an overseas oil agreement". It is pointed out that the knowledge of boundaries is absolutely essential and now presumed – without the intention of a corruptive behavior it will still be punished; on the other hand exceptions exist as well:

> *"The overseas subsidiary of an UK oil company is bidding for a production sharing agreement with a North African country. It has been made clear to the bidders that the government would expect 'planning gain' with facilities to be provided for the local community to compensate it for the disruption of extraction and piping but also to counter any unrest adverse to the government because local communities will not benefit from the revenues. An amount of several million dollars for a hospital has been suggested. The payment for the community facility would be made as a donation to a charitable trust to be nominated by the minister for energy. No details of*

[117] Wilkinson, Peter: "The 2010 UK Bribery Act Adequate Procedures", Transparency International (2010), Pg.7

the trust have been provided so far nor how the payment would be made.

Key issues to note

The UK oil company could be liable under section 6 of the Bribery Act if its subsidiary were to be judged as providing

an advantage at the request or with the assent or acquiescence of a foreign public official;

The advantage would be to the charitable trust and/or government politicians as they would be enhanced in their ability to stay in office and to avoid community unrest;

It could also be an offence under section 7 of failure to prevent bribery as the donation for a hospital might be an inducement to the government to award the contract improperly;

There is a risk to the company if the charitable trust has officers or involvement by public officials or their families; and - It will not be an offence under section 6 (or section 7) if permitted by written law."

Comment

The company should have a clear public policy for planning gain solicitations including that the planning gain has a valid business rationale e.g., if environmental or community adverse impact or loss will result from the contract; the planning gain process should be transparent and include public planning review. Due diligence should be carried out on the body to which the funds are to be paid to check whether any public officials are involved and that the funds will not be applied to another purpose."[118]

Relating to this example a certain complexity becomes more obvious. Training and education are the crucial key factors to provide a successful implementation firstly in U.K. itself and then possibly EU directives may be applied to duplicate the core essence and adapt it to the other countries or even supranational.

---

[118] Wilkinson, Peter: "The 2010 UK Bribery Act Adequate Procedures", Transparency International (2010), Pg. 47

8.2 Code of Conduct – Lessons (to be) Learned

There are numerous factors that have to considered when anti-corruption efforts should be successful. The TI Source Book "Confronting Corruption: The Elements of a National Integrity System" states 39 of those.[119]

> *"**18 Access to information***
> *Some governments have recognized transparent access to information as the most effective tool for curbing corruption and have enacted appropriate legislation. Government agencies can be required to post details of the services they provide and the official charges for them. Indonesia is an example where local information displays with details of development projects have equipped the public with the information they need to keep a watchful eye on what is taking place."*[120]

Ironically Indonesia is still a hub of corruption which indicated that a positive enactment of only a few of those "steps" are not sufficient in any way, as the elusive nature of corruption consequently just exploits differently.

Furthermore the conducting of methods is the key component to realization when a spot on implementation was performed. A new legislature is again *not sufficient* alone – monitoring processes, evaluating scope of immunities, observing public auctions, maintaining international agreements and especially black listing of known corrupted firms is indispensable.

The last necessity is fiercely disputed and fought by lobbies. Actually a great number of huge businesses were multiple times convicted of collusion, bribery, fraud etc. and still mostly they are fined with penalties that do not exceed their "risk/opportunity cost" which leads to a continuation of being overly risk prone.

---

[119] Pope, Jeremy: "Confronting Corruption: The Elements of a National Integrity System", Transparency International (2000), TI Source Book, Pg. 295-302

[120] Pope, Jeremy: "Confronting Corruption: The Elements of a National Integrity System", Transparency International (2000), TI Source Book, Pg. 299

9. Recap

As the effects of corruption are difficult to determine, define and recognize to their full extent, the environment has to be analyzed regularly and the scope of research has to enlarge from regional to national matters and finally supranational systems have to classified and evaluated.
The greater part of the world is according to the CPI still in need of a greater transition to a less corruption polluted environment. Regarding respect, responsibility and reliability as attributes a new movement, induced by anti-corruption boards and directives, is proceeding in Europe and parts of the U.S. towards a more stable future in energy and less corruption overall.

It is crucial to maintain this (minor) positive tendency with quick and responsive regulatory boards to prevent speculation and financial mismanagement for the sake of a steady supply of energy throughout society.
Considering insights of the cases privatization of the power sector is not a quick way of healing financial wounds as the beneficial part of these markets may only come into existence with adapted and appropriate regulatory mechanisms and institutes.

Tightly government controlled sectors may also be inefficient concerning irresponsive and perhaps even defiled agencies, that are decadent and dismissive of progress in society and technological advancements.
Examples for clean firms in the energy sector in the home country and abroad would be the Austrian multicorporate enterprise "Verbund"[121] and the Swedish conglomerate "Vattenfall" with multiple operations internationally and a sustainable growth and stability. Firms tend to operate differently abroad as explained in the chapters before.[122]

---

[121] As a side remark: Verbund has left its markets which are not consistent with their maxim: http://www.verbund.com/cc/de/news-presse/news/2011/07/27/verbund-verkauft-anteil-an-poweo (last accessed on 22.02.2012)

[122] Hardoon, Deborah; Heinrich, Finn: "Bribe Payers Index 2011", Transparency International (2011), Pg. 15

California is just the most prominent case study in matters of corruption and also in particular for a quick regulation change with a nearly full liberalization in a state that was known prior for its precarious law enforcement – it failed miserably as the loopholes provoked corruption.

A further positive progress in markets (which are quite complicated nationally and internationally for the production, transfer and distribution of energy resources) are achieved by enactment of effectively enforceable laws.

If a public sector was corrupt before the privatization the probability of a continuing persistence is high.[123]

Another huge factor seems to be the accountability of the firm and its members. A lack of penalties leads nearly automatically to a recklessness of the participants of the market and unnecessary risky actions. If nothing is learned from mistakes a reoccurrence is almost certain.

For instance the oil speculation case of Enron in 1987 throws quite a big shadow on the downfall of 2001 and draws a direct line to it, but apparently not for the regulators or other policy makers.[124]

In summary, it can be stated that history repeats itself, ignorance of the "lessons to be learned" results in various ways of inefficiency and that corruption produces more costs than the profit of the few beneficiaries, as shown in the preceding chosen cases. The regulation theory must be adapted by the functions outside of the model - especially in supranational consisting way - certain used practices, political environment, interferences of the financial market and numerous circumstances in other markets to prevent abusive behavior.[125]

Lastly the importance of valid and reliable scientific methods has to be underlined as an alarmingly great amount of estimations in the energy sector are neglecting those attributes, which results in a corrupted state of "knowledge" and leads to illogical decisions, deceiving politics and misinvestments.

---

[123] http://online.wsj.com/article/SB10001424052702304432704577347801235907294.html (last accessed on 22.02.2013)

[124] http://www.washingtonpost.com/wp-dyn/content/article/2005/11/04/AR2005110401710.html (last accessed on 16.06.2013)

[125] Fortelny, Marc-Joël: "When and how is regulation circumvented in the energy market?", University of Vienna (2013), Pg. 20-21

Abstract

The objective of this study is to depict the energy environment regarding the various sources of energy, the correlation of energy mixes, various trends of transition and mainly corruption of these preceding aspects. An insight of successful and failing counter-measures is also provided.

Along the analysis of numerous case studies a focus on "Extracted Key Factors" of the explored and evaluated characteristics of corruption and the energy sector is placed upon. The term corruption in an economic environment is defined as fraud, bribery, immorality and misuse of power, however the actual scope is greater, as the interdependencies of nations, economies and their corresponding interactions create disruptions and discrepancies – especially when lobbying is exploited. Misinformation and the corruption of data are the most difficult research topics, as science should not be misused in forcing an opinion with falsifying facts for instance and must not lead to technical provable contradictions.

The approach to fight corruption is most likely to be efficient and successful if performed supranational on all public sectors - with adaptations to the energy sector - by all means with high collaborative efforts.

Zusammenfassung

Das Ziel dieser Forschung ist es die Umwelt des Energiesektors hinsichtlich der verschiedenen Quellen von Energie, der Korrelation von Energie Portfolios, verschiedener Trends von Übergängen und hauptsächlich der Korruption dieser vorangegangen Aspekte darzustellen. Ein Einblick in erfolgreiche und versagende Gegenmaßnahmen wird ebenfalls gewährt.

Zusammen mit der Analyse von zahlreichen Fallstudien wird ein Fokus auf die "Extrahierten Schlüssel Faktoren" der erforschten und evaluierten Charakteristika von Korruption und Energiesektor gelegt. Der Begriff Korruption in einem ökonomischen Umfeld wird durch Betrug, Bestechung, Immoralität and Missbrauch von Macht definiert, jedoch ist das tatsächliche Betrachtungsfeld größer, da die Interdependenzen der Nationen, Ökonomien und deren kennzeichnende Interaktionen Störungen und Diskrepanzen erzeugen – im Speziellen wenn "Lobbying" (aus)genutzt wird. Fehlinformation und die Korrumpierung von Daten sind die problematischsten Themen, da die Wissenschaft als solche nicht missbraucht werden darf um eine Meinung, beispielsweise mit verfälschten Fakten, zu erzwingen und nicht zu technisch überprüfbaren Widersprüchen führen darf.

Eine Vorgehensweise bei der Bekämpfung von Korruption ist am wahrscheinlichsten effizient und erfolgreich, wenn sie supranational in allen öffentlichen Bereichen - mit Anpassungen im Energiesektor - jedenfalls mit hohen kollaborativen Anstrengungen erfolgt.

List of Literature

Brauetigam, Roland; Panzar, John: „Effects of the Change from Rate-of-Return to Price-Cap Regulation" American Economic Association (1993) The American Economic Review Vol. 83, No. 2, Papers and Proceedings of the Hundred and Fifth Annual Meeting of the American Economic Association

Deakin, Simon: "Learning from Enron" University of Cambridge (2003)Working Paper No. 274

Fortelny, Marc-Joël: "When and how is regulation circumvented in the energy market?", University of Vienna (2013)

Fortelny, Marc-Joël: „Unavowed aspects of the Financial Crisis and its aftermath / bottom (-) line", University of Vienna (2012)

Fox, Loren: "Enron: The Rise and Fall", John Wiley&Sons (2003)

Hardoon, Deborah; Heinrich, Finn: "Bribe Payers Index 2011", Transparency International (2011)

Healy, Paul M. and Palepu, Krishna G.: "The Fall of Enron" Journal of Economic Perspectives – Volume 17, Number2 ,(Spring 2003) , Pg. 3-26

Kilian, Lutz: "The Economic Effects of Energy Price Shocks", University of Michigan (2007)

McLean, Bethany; Elkind, Peter : "The Smartest Guys in the Room: The Amazing Rise and Scandalous Fall of Enron" Portfolio Trade (2004) Reprint

Pope, Jeremy: "Confronting Corruption: The Elements of a National Integrity System", Transparency International (2000), TI Source Book

Ralston, Jonah J.: ""Peak Oil": The eventual end of the oil age", Washington University in St. Louis (2008), Doctoral Thesis

Slocum, Tyson: "The Failure of Electricity Deregulation: History, Status and Needed Reforms", Public Citizen´s Energy Program (2007)

Viscusi, W. Kip; Harrington, Joseph E. Jr; Vernon, John M.: „Economics of Regulation and Antitrust", MIT Press (1995) Fourth Edition

Wilkinson, Peter: "The 2010 UK Bribery Act Adequate Procedures", Transparency International (2010)

Internet Sources

http://goo.gl/XAKhQ (last accessed on 24.05.2013)

http://business.baylor.edu/Tom_kelly/Californial%20Power.htm (last accessed on 22.02.2013)

http://www.risk.net/energy-risk/feature/2232244/academic-battle-rages-over-oil-speculation-high-prices-and-volatility (last accessed on 22.02.2013)

http://www.valueline.com/Stocks/Commentary.aspx?id=13098 (last accessed on 22.02.2013)

http://www.mcclatchydc.com/2012/02/21/139521/once-again-speculators-behind.html (last accessed on 22.02.2013)

http://www.ftc.gov/bcp/workshops/energymarkets/background/slocum_dereg.pdf (last accessed on 22.02.2013)

http://www.businessdictionary.com/definition/corruption.html (last accessed on 16.06.2013)

http://www.europarl.europa.eu/document/activities/cont/201206/20120626ATT47717/20120626ATT47717EN.pdf (last accessed on 16.06.2013)

http://www.health24.com/Lifestyle/Environmental-health/News/Wind-farm-potential-overestimated-20130227 (last accessed on 16.06.2013)

http://transparency.org/whoweare/history (last accessed on 16.06.2013)

http://www.focus.de/finanzen/news/verfahren-wegen-preisabsprachen-kartoffel-kartell-prellte-verbaucher-und-bauern-um-eine-milliarde-euro_aid_986263.html (last accessed on 16.06.2013)

http://live.worldbank.org/monitoring-results-performance-indicators-enforcement-anticorruption-laws (last accessed on 16.06.2013)

http://jia.sipa.columbia.edu/russia%E2%80%99s-financial-crisis-economic-setbacks-and-policy-responses (last accessed on 16.06.2013)

http://regulationbodyofknowledge.org/price-level-regulation/features-of-price-cap-and-revenue-cap-regulation/ (last accessed on 22.02.2013)

http://regulationbodyofknowledge.org/price-level-regulation/properties-of-benchmarking-and-yardstick-regulation/ (last accessed on 22.02.2013)

http://warrington.ufl.edu/centers/purc/purcdocs/papers/0213_sappington_price_regulation_and.pdf (last accessed on 22.02.2013)

http://visual.ly/american-energy-spectrum?view=true (last accessed on 24.02.2013)

http://www.central2013.eu/typo3temp/pics/003eca7911.jpg (last accessed on 15.06.2013)

http://visual.ly/europes-power-shift (last accessed on 15.06.2013) http://blueandgreentomorrow.com/features/infographic-renewable-energy-in-europe/ (last accessed on 15.06.2013)

http://transparency.org/research (last accessed on 15.06.2013)

http://cpi.transparency.org/cpi2012/in_detail/ (last accessed on 15.06.2013)

http://cpi.transparency.org/cpi2012/ (last accessed on 15.06.2013)

http://cpi.transparency.org/cpi2012/results/ (last accessed on 15.06.2013)

http://rt.com/politics/scandal-corruption-putin-energy-488/ (last accessed on 15.06.2013)

http://www.igidr.ac.in/faculty/nag/FDI%20in%20India%20in%20the%201990s.pdf (last accessed on 15.06.2013

http://visual.ly/cost-corruption (last accessed on 15.06.2013)

http://www.ferc.gov/industries/electric/indus-act/wec/chron/chronology.pdf (last accessed on 22.02.2013)

http://www.ferc.gov/industries/electric/indus-act/wec/enron/summary-findings.pdf(last accessed on 22.02.2013)

http://www.oib.gov.tr/tedas/teaser_english.pdf (last accessed on 22.02.2013)

http://www.tedas.gov.tr/Sayfalar/Anasayfa.aspx (last accessed on 22.02.2013)

http://www.todayszaman.com/newsDetail_getNewsById.action?load=detay&link=218239 (last accessed on 22.02.2013)

http://online.wsj.com/article/SB10001424052702304432704577347801235907294.html (last accessed on 22.02.2013)

http://www.nytimes.com/2013/01/31/business/global/dutch-court-rules-shell-partly-responsible-for-nigerian-spills.html?pagewanted=all&_r=0 (last accessed on 16.06.2013)

http://siteresources.worldbank.org/INTENERGY2/Resources/electricitsourcebookch8.pdf (last accessed on 22.02.2013)

http://www.theatlantic.com/business/archive/2013/03/americas-most-obvious-tax-reform-idea-kill-the-oil-and-gas-subsidies/274121/ (last accessed on 16.06.2013)

www.forbes.com/sites/tomkonrad/2011/05/24/financial-innovation-is-blowin-in-the-wind/ (last accessed on 22.02.2013)

http://www.justice.gov/opa/pr/2003/March/03_crm_153.htm (last accessed on 22.02.2013)

http://caraellison.wordpress.com/2009/09/14/cnn-misrepresents-enrons-weather-futures/ (last accessed on 22.02.2013)

http://www.wired.com/techbiz/media/news/2001/11/48732?currentPage=all (last accessed on 22.02.2013)

http://www.worldcoal.org/coal/where-is-coal-found/ (last accessed on 24.08.2012) http://controlgrowth.org/double.htm cross reference of Dr. Bartlett (last accessed on 24.08.2012)

http://www.geo.cornell.edu/eas/energy/_Media/mkh_oil.jpeg (last accessed on 16.06.2013)

http://lindseynicholson.org/wp-content/uploads/2012/09/energy-comparison.jpg (last accessed on 16.06.2013)

http://www.appliedmaterials.com/sites/default/files/infographic_730w_1_0.jpg (last accessed on 15.06.2013)

http://www.shell.com/global/environment-society/ecomarathon/events/americas/fan-zone/highlights/student-energy-challenge.html (last accessed on 16.06.2013)

http://www.forbes.com/sites/energysource/2010/07/07/14-efficiency-for-thin-film-solar-cells-but-where-will-the-indium-come-from/ (last accessed 16.06.2013)

http://www.greatenergychallengeblog.com/2013/06/06/student-infographic-contest-paints-bright-picture-of-youth-concern-on-energy-and-climate/ (last accessed 16.06.2013)
http://www.opensecrets.org/lobby/indus.php?id=E (last accessed on 16.06.2013)

http://www.businessdictionary.com/definition/lobbying.html (last accessed on 16.06.2013)

http://pdf.usaid.gov/pdf_docs/PNACT875.pdf (last accessed on 22.02.2013)

http://www.renewableenergyworld.com/rea/news/article/2010/12/top-25-u-s-energy-lobbyists-of-2010 (last accessed on 16.06.2013)

http://www.verbund.com/cc/de/news-presse/news/2011/07/27/verbund-verkauft-anteil-an-poweo (last accessed on 22.02.2012)

http://online.wsj.com/article/SB10001424052702304432704577347801235907294.html (last accessed on 22.02.2013)

http://www.washingtonpost.com/wp-dyn/content/article/2005/11/04/AR2005110401710.html (last accessed on 16.06.2013)

Appendices

Appendix 1

7,18	7,18
7,3954	14,5754
7,617262	22,19266
7,84578	30,03844
8,081153	38,1196
8,323588	46,44318
8,573295	55,01648
8,830494	63,84697
9,095409	72,94238
9,368271	82,31065
9,64932	91,95997
9,938799	101,8988
10,23696	112,1357
10,54407	122,6798
10,86039	133,5402
11,18621	144,7264
11,52179	156,2482
11,86745	168,1156
12,22347	180,3391
12,59017	192,9293
12,96788	205,8972

year 0-1 > base rate and first year accumulated consumption sum

847 billion tons estimated total amount for 118 years

7,18 tons per year current rate

Steady growth of 3 %

13,35692	219,2541	
13,75762	233,0117	
14,17035	247,1821	<= doubling time of 23 years approximately
14,59546	261,7775	
15,03333	276,8108	
15,48433	292,2952	
15,94886	308,244	
16,42732	324,6713	
16,92014	341,5915	
17,42774	359,0192	
17,95058	376,9698	
18,48909	395,4589	
19,04377	414,5027	
19,61508	434,1177	
20,20353	454,3213	
20,80964	475,1309	
21,43393	496,5648	
22,07695	518,6418	
22,73925	541,381	
23,42143	564,8025	
24,12407	588,9266	
24,8478	613,7743	
25,59323	639,3676	
26,36103	665,7286	

27,15186	692,8805		
27,96641	720,8469	<=	quadrupling time of 46 years approximately
28,80541	749,6523		
29,66957	779,3219		
30,55966	809,8815		
31,47645	841,358		
32,42074	873,7787	<=	resources of 847 billion tons of coal are depleted in 51 years
rate/year	acc. Sum		